JOURNAL OF LEGAL PLURALISM
and Unofficial Law

NUMBER 59 / 2009

Bibliographic information published by the Deutsche Nationalbibliothek
The Deutsche Nationalbibliothek lists this publication in the Deutsche Nationalbibliografie; detailed bibliographic data are available in the Internet at http://dnb.d-nb.de.

ISSN 0732-9113
ISBN 978-3-643-99917-7

A catalogue record for this book is available from the British Library

Fresnostr. 2 D-48159 Münster
Tel. +49 (0) 2 51-620 320 Fax +49 (0) 2 51-922 60 99
e-Mail: lit@lit-verlag.de http://www.lit-verlag.de

Distribution:

In Germany: LIT Verlag Fresnostr. 2, D-48159 Münster
Tel. +49 (0) 2 51-620 32 22, Fax +49 (0) 2 51-922 60 99, e-mail: vertrieb@lit-verlag.de

In Austria: Medienlogistik Pichler-ÖBZ, e-mail: mlo@medien-logistik.at

In Switzerland: B + M Buch- und Medienvertrieb, e-mail: order@buch-medien.ch

In the UK: Global Book Marketing, e-mail: mo@centralbooks.com

In North America by:

Transaction Publishers
New Brunswick (U.S.A.) and London (U.K.)

Transaction Publishers
Rutgers University
35 Berrue Circle
Piscataway, NJ 08854

Phone: +1 (732) 445 - 2280
Fax: + 1 (732) 445 - 3138
for orders (U. S. only):
toll free (888) 999 - 6778
e-mail: orders@transactionpub.com

JOURNAL OF LEGAL PLURALISM
and Unofficial Law

POLICY

The Journal of Legal Pluralism and Unofficial Law (JLP) is a refereed, independent, inter-disciplinary, international journal devoted to scholarly writing, documentation, information on current developments, and communications about all aspects of legal pluralism and unofficial law anywhere in the world and at any time. Issues 1-18 bear the name *African Law Studies*.

MANUSCRIPTS

Manuscripts for the Journal of Legal Pluralism should be submitted to the editor-in-chief:

Gordon R. Woodman
School of Law, University of Birmingham
Edgbaston, Birmingham B15 2TT
United Kingdom
Fax: (+ 44) (0)121 414 3585
Email: G.R.Woodman@bham.ac.uk

or to one of the associate editors. Unless the editors are otherwise informed, submission of a manuscript implies the undertaking that it is not currently being considered by another journal and that if accepted it will be available for publication.

Manuscripts must conform to the style and other instructions contained in the JLP 'style sheet' (to be found on the JLP web site under the title 'Author guidelines'), and should generally be submitted in electronic form.

SUBSCRIPTIONS

Subscriptions to the Journal of Legal Pluralism are currently □29.90 per number for individuals. Two numbers are published each year, the two amounting to approximately 200 pages. From nr. 49 (2004) the Journal has been published by LIT Verlag, Münster-Hamburg-Berlin-Vienna-London, whose address for orders is Grevener St./Fresnostr.2, D-48159 Münster, Germany, Fax (+49) (0)251 23 19 72, vertrieb@lit-verlag.de.
Back numbers of African Law Studies and the Journal of Legal Pluralism to nr. 48 are available from William S. Hein & Co., Inc., 1285 Main Street, Buffalo, New York 14209-1987, USA..

INDEXES AND DATABASES

Articles appearing in the Journal of Legal Pluralism are indexed in the principal legal and social science indexes and online data-bases. It is planned to make available the full text of all articles published more than two years previously on the website of the Journal of Legal Pluralism at www.jlp.bham.ac.uk . Currently the site contains the full text of all articles in nrs. 20 to 54, and abstracts of articles in nrs. 43 to the current number.

CITATION

The Journal of Legal Pluralism and Unofficial Law should be cited as: *Journal of Legal Pluralism*.

CONTENTS

BOOK REVIEWS

FROM THE EDITORS

As usual the papers in this number of the *JLP* examine a number of social settings which vary widely, both in their geographic locations and in their cultural characteristics. The methodologies used by authors also vary, ranging from different forms of social-empirical research to analysis of written court records.

Three of the six articles (by Wang Qiliang, Corrin and Nielsen) have been developed from papers given at conferences of the Commission on Legal Pluralism (formerly the Commission on Folk Law and Legal Pluralism) of the International Union of Anthropological and Ethnological Sciences. The *JLP* has maintained close relations with the Commission since it was founded. The next number will be a special number consisting of articles developed from papers given at the Commission conference in Zurich in 2009, prepared by Guest Editor Yüksel Sezgin. The following number will contain a section consisting of papers developed from the same conference, prepared by Fauzia Shariff. Although this is exceptional – a substantial number of papers not in this category are currently in the processes of review and editorial preparation – it is beneficial for the *JLP*, since the conferences encourage the preparation of papers by scholars and practitioners who have many different foci of interest, but who are united in believing that the notion of legal pluralism may prove to be illuminating for their different concerns. The current website of the Commission may be visited at http://www.commission-on-legal-pluralism.ch/.

Another on-line resource which readers of the JLP may find useful is that of Droits de l'homme et dialogue interculturel/ Human Rights and Intercultural Dialogue at http://www.dhdi.org, managed by Christoph Eberhard.

Gordon Woodman

ABSTRACTS OF ARTICLES

***JLP* 59: 1-27**

RELIGION, LEGAL PLURALISM AND ORDER IN A MULTIETHNIC SOCIETY: A LEGAL-ANTHROPOLOGICAL STUDY IN CONTEMPORARY CHINA

Wang Qiliang

Religion, as a kind of social control, plays a role in the construction of social order. It contributes to shaping or influencing the formation of local legal culture, to the generation of various norms, and to the production of social controllers, and it affects dispute settlement. Religious social control in the social grass-roots of China has developed an intricate form as a result of the interaction between plural religions and multi-ethnicity, which in turn speeds up the formation of legal pluralism. This article, based on the analysis of specific cases and ethnographic materials, examines the dynamic relationship between religion, the state law and other social controls within the perspective of legal pluralism. The paper also discusses whether religion will destroy or hinder the process of building legal unity in the multiethnic society of China.

***JLP* 59: 29-48**

MOVING BEYOND THE HIERARCHICAL APPROACH TO LEGAL PLURALISM IN THE SOUTH PACIFIC

Jennifer Corrin

In countries of the South Pacific, societies are often discussed in terms of the dichotomy between 'traditional' and 'modern'. Similarly, legal systems are often described by reference to the dichotomy between 'customary' or 'traditional' law and 'state law', and between 'informal' and 'formal' justice. In fact, these divisions are becoming a thing of the past, gradually blurred by changes in the pattern of society and by the interaction between different systems of law. Further, the approach taken to the accommodation of customary law, which has been to formally 'recognise' it in constitutions, has, at least in theory, put an end to its independent operation. In the search for a more effective approach to legal pluralism, the existing dichotomy may often obscure a more complex interplay between the interwoven spheres of 'traditional law' and 'state law' and a new sphere of 'blended' law. In each of these spheres there are uncertainties, including questions of definition and scope, which constitute a potentially destabilising factor and have significant rule of law implications.

Commencing with an overview of the different sources and types of law within the 'customary' and 'state' law spheres in the South Pacific region, this paper discusses some of the uncertainties and tensions that arise from pluralism in practice. Examples drawn mainly from Solomon Islands are used to illustrate the various ways in which the lines between customary law and state law have been blurred. These include attempts to incorporate customary law in statutes. Two examples of statutes which provide for this are considered, and the case-law arising from them is discussed.

***JLP* 59: 49-65**

'GOD IS AN ABSENTEE, TOO': THE TREATMENT OF *WAQF* (ISLAMIC TRUST) LAND IN ISRAEL/PALESTINE

Haitam Suleiman and Robert Home

Waqf property (held in charitable trust for religious purposes) has been an important element in Muslim societies, and after a period of decline has emerged as a non-profit 'third' sector for minorities and in conditions of legal pluralism. This article, after briefly tracing the history of *waqf*, examines the large-scale transfer of *waqf* land in Israel/Palestine to Jewish control since the creation of the state of Israel in 1948, and places that confiscation within a context of postcolonial legal pluralism. The role of successive Absentee Property Laws in this confiscation is related to Ottoman land tenure categories and the Ottoman Land Code, as modified under the British League of Nations Mandate. The special legal status of *waqf* in the Old City of Jerusalem is discussed, and recent legal disputes over the status of certain mosques and cemeteries are examined as sites of resistance.

***JLP* 59: 67-85**

DISTINCTION WITHOUT DIFFERENCE: THE CONSTITUTIONAL PROTECTION OF CUSTOMARY LAW AND CULTURAL, LINGUISTIC AND RELIGIOUS COMMUNITIES – A COMMENT ON *SHILUBANA & OTHERS v NWAMITWA*

E.S. Nwauche

The decision of the South African Constitutional Court in *Shilubana and Others v Nwamitwa* ([2008] ZACC 9 (CC), the *Shilubana* case) appears to herald a more sympathetic understanding of customary law, but it also reveals the fact that customary law applies exclusively to the black community in South Africa while other racial communities are imagined and protected in terms of the rights in sections 30 and 31 of the Final Constitution (FC). This paper contends that this distinction is not only wrong but of no significant difference. It is further contended that protection of all racial communities should proceed on the basis of sections 30 and 31 of the FC because the framework of these two sections appears better suited for the protection of all communities if South African courts show a more sympathetic understanding of communal norms and institutions. This comment argues that the *Shilubana* case is a tentative but welcome example of this trend. In the case the CC upheld a decision of the Valoyi Tribe to appoint a woman as a traditional leader. This was a development of its customary law of traditional succession that had hitherto operated on the basis of male primogeniture. In recognizing a gender neutral traditional leadership institution, the Court demonstrated that institutions established by communal norms can exist and function on the basis of equality and other rights which are the hallmarks of a liberal constitution.

With reference to that decision this comment undertakes an overview of group rights in the FC. It considers the exclusive association of customary law with the 'black' community and questions whether this association has enhanced the group rights of the black community. It assesses the interpretation of the rights of members of cultural, linguistic and religious communities under sections 30 and 31 of the FC as interpreted in the *Shilubana* case and other cases to ascertain how far they advance group rights. It concludes by urging a unified interpretation of 'communities' and a more beneficial interpretation of 'group rights' that recognizes that all racial groups have their own customary laws and deserve a more sensitive recognition of their communal norms.

***JLP* 59: 87-120**

THE POLITICS OF LEGAL PLURALISM: STATE POLICIES ON LEGAL PLURALISM AND THEIR LOCAL DYNAMICS IN MOZAMBIQUE

Helene Maria Kyed

What happens when *legal pluralism* becomes a policy concept? Or put differently: what are the consequences when legal pluralism enters national laws and policies and thereby ceases to be solely an analytical concept used by scholars to address the plurality of normative orders and institutions that enforce order within a political organisation? This article explores the consequences of legal pluralism as a policy concept, and argues that it is of utmost importance to acknowledge how policies on legal pluralism can give way to different layers of politics in practice. Such 'politics of legal pluralism' denotes the, often covert, political interests behind legal pluralism policies and the political implications of how such policies are put into effect. Despite official discourse, the article argues, legal pluralism as a policy concept seldom alone implies a benign recognition of the empirical manifestations of socio-cultural diversity. It also implies a framework for state intervention, regulation and reform, which has political implications. Legal pluralism policies easily become subject to political manipulation or may be political tools in themselves to assert authority and manifest power by state and non-state actors. At the heart of the issue is the fact that justice enforcement, and by extension social ordering, are not neutral, apolitical activities, but political ones: they provide a route to authority and also often to an income.

The article draws on the case of Mozambique where legal pluralism has been recognised in the 2004 Constitution, and where a range of state efforts to recognise non-state justice and policing providers have taken place since the civil war ended in 1992. Based on extensive fieldwork since 2002, the article explores the state recognition of traditional authorities in rural areas and the more recent implementation of community policing in urban areas. With these examples, the article shows that the politics of legal pluralism can take the form of at least three layers of politics, but also recognises that these may vary according to context: i.e. the politics of asserting the superior authority of state institutions and law over other existing legal orders or through the establishment of new non-state institutions; the political party interests in controlling non-state legal orders to consolidate power; and local level contestations over power and 'clients' to sustain the authority of a given institution or of personal power positions. In Mozambique the result of these layers of politics is new forms of plurality, but these co-exist with, and are reshaped by, state and regime efforts to monopolise the legal domain, even to such an extent that the very notion of 'pluralism' itself is under constant attack.

***JLP* 59: 121-144**

FARMERS' USE OF THE COURTS IN AN ANTI-LAND ACQUISITION MOVEMENT IN INDIA'S WEST BENGAL

Kenneth Bo Nielsen

In 2006 Singur in West Bengal, India, was chosen as the location for a new far factory that was to produce what would ostensibly become the world's cheapest car. To make way for the factory approximately 1,000 acres of farmland were expropriated by the state government. Farmers unwilling to relinquish their land refused to comply with the acquisition and organised politically to challenge the legitimacy, both moral and legal, of the government's exercise of the right of eminent domain. While these farmers relied on a broad repertoire of contention during their prolonged agitation, the courts and the law provided them with perhaps the most important arena for challenging the state. This paper discusses various aspects of the Singur farmers' use of the courts, asking: (1) How have the farmers in practice gone about accessing the courts and the legal system? (2) What has been their experience of engaging with such a complex system of procedures and institutions that rely on a language with which few farmers are familiar? (3) Given that many other options have been available, why have the Singur farmers chosen to repose such faith in the courts?

ABOUT THE CONTRIBUTORS

Judith BEYER is a Research Fellow in the Project Group Legal Pluralism at the Max-Planck-Institute for Social Anthropology, Halle. See further the section 'About the Contributors' in nr. 53/54 of the *Journal of Legal Pluralism*.

Jennifer CORRIN is Executive Director, Asia Pacific Law, Centre for Public, International and Comparative Law and Associate Professor, TC Beirne School of Law, The University of Queensland. After taking Bachelor's and Master's degrees in law she practised as a solicitor in England. She later qualified as a Barrister in Queensland, and then as a Barrister and Solicitor in Solomon Islands and Fiji. She gained a PhD at Griffith University in 2003. She was formerly Associate Professor of Law at the University of the South Pacific in Vanuatu. Her publications include: (with J. Zorn) *Proving Customary Law in the Common Law Courts of the South Pacific*. London: British Institute of International and Comparative Law (2002); *Civil Procedure and Courts in the South Pacific*. London: Cavendish Publishing, 2004; (with D. Paterson) *Introduction to South Pacific Law,* 2nd edn. Abingdon: Routledge-Cavendish (2007).

Robert HOME is Professor in Land Management at the Law School, Anglia Ruskin University, Chelmsford, United Kingdom. After completing his Ph.D. in Geography at the London School of Economics, he qualified as a chartered town planner, and has published widely on land and planning law. He has edited (with Hilary Lim) *Demystifying the Mystery of Capital: Land in Africa and the Caribbean*. London: Routledge-Cavendish (2004). He has written articles on land law in Israel/Palestine in *Planning Perspectives* and *Socio-Legal Studies*, and contributed to international expert group meetings on Islamic land law.

Amy JACKSON is a Ph.D. candidate of the University of Reading, funded by the Graduate Schools of Social Sciences and Arts and Humanities. She has gained an LLB degree from the University of Reading after a course which included a period at Uppsala Universet, Sweden under the ERASMUS year abroad program. She gained an LLM from the University of Sussex for a dissertation entitled *How Might Legal Pluralist Methods Lead to a Better Understanding of the role of Other Actors in Public International Law*? The aim of her Ph.D. thesis is to consider a critical legal pluralist approach to the debate surrounding the choice of women to wear the Islamic veil.

Helene Maria KYED is currently a project researcher at the Danish Institute for International Studies. Born in Denmark, she has a Master Honours degree in Social Anthropology from the University of Aarhus and a PhD degree in International Development Studies from the University of Roskilde. Her publications include: (edited with Lars Buur) *State Recognition and Democratization in Sub-Saharan Africa. A New Dawn for Traditional Authorities?* Basingstoke: Palgrave-Macmillan (2007); (with Lars Buur and Terezinha C. Silva) *State Recognition of Local Authorities and Public Participation: Experiences, Obstacles and Possibilities in Mozambique*. Maputo: Ministry of Justice and Danish Institute for International Studies (2007). She has also published articles in *Development and Change*, *Policing and Society* and the *Journal of Southern African Studies* on traditional authority, citizenship, sovereignty and local forms of justice enforcement and policing. She has conducted long-term fieldwork in Mozambique on the state recognition of traditional authorities and the interaction between state and non-state justice and security providers. Particularly, Kyed has addressed the political implications of state-non-state engagements, and addressed theoretical questions concerning competing forms of sovereignty, social ordering and claims to authority. Her current research also engages with the topic of community policing in Sub-Saharan Africa.

Christian LUND is Professor in International Development Studies at Roskilde University. For close to two decades he has worked on land and politics issues in West Africa, primarily in Niger, Ghana and Burkina Faso, with a particular interest in local politics and conflicts over natural resources. He is currently commencing research on similar issues in Laos. He has been a Visiting Scholar at University of California, Berkeley, London School of Economics, Centre for Development Research, Copenhagen, and École des Hautes Études en Sciences Sociales (School of Advanced Social Studies) in Marseille. His principal recent publications include: (edited) *Twilight Institutions. Public Authority and Local Politics in Africa*. Oxford: Wiley-Blackwell (2007); *Local Politics and the Dynamics of Property in Africa*. Cambridge and New York: Cambridge University Press (2008); (edited with Thomas Sikor) *The Politics of Possession: Property, Authority, and Access to Natural Resources*. London: Wiley-Blackwell (2009). In addition to other books which he has written and edited he has published in journals such as *Africa*, *Development and Change*, *Journal of Modern African Studies, and World Development.*

L. Jane McMILLAN holds the Canada Research Chair in Indigenous Peoples and Sustainable Communities at the Department of Anthropology, St. Francis Xavier University, Antigonish, Nova Scotia, Canada. She holds a Master's degree from Dalhousie University and a PhD from the University of British Columbia. She is a legal anthropologist with a specialization in Indigenous justice. Her recent works explore the impact of colonization on traditional law ways of the Mi'kmaq of eastern Canada and their contemporary community responses to legal issues. Her current community-based, participatory action collaborative research includes a programme on 'Aboriginal Family Violence – creating meaningful community responses to intimate violence'.

Kenneth Bo NIELSEN is a Research Fellow at SUM (Centre for Development and the Environment, University of Oslo), Norway, and chief consultant at KL (Local Government Denmark). He obtained his Cand. Scient. degree (MA equivalent) in anthropology from the University of Copenhagen in 2005 with a thesis was on urban Indian middle class youth and the Indian state and politics. He then worked on a minor research project on the religious organisation of the Indian Hindu Diaspora in Copenhagen. His current Ph.D. project has the working title: "In Defence of the Land: Rural Social Movements and Urban Activists in India's West Bengal." It analyses the making of a rural social movement opposing government-directed forced land acquisition in the Indian state of West Bengal. His recent publications are: '"Not on our land!" Peasants' Struggle against Forced Land Acquisition in India's West Bengal.' Pp. 217-46 in Dan Banik (ed.), *Rights and Legal Empowerment in Eradicating Poverty*. Farnham: Ashgate (2008); 'Contesting India's Development? Industrialisation, Land Acquisition and Protest in West Bengal.' *Forum for Development Studies* 37: 145-70 (2010).

Enyinna S. NWAUCHE is Associate Professor of Law at Rivers State University of Science and Technology, Port Harcourt, Nigeria. He is also Director of the Centre for African Legal Studies, a research based advocacy centre dedicated to exploring how African countries have articulated, developed and maintained normative systems which govern their lives. He holds an LLM from Obafemi Awolowo University, Nigeria His recent publications include: "The Dubious Distinction between Principal and Accessory Claims in Nigerian Human Rights Jurisprudence." *Journal of African Law* 52: 66-88 (2008); "Law Religion and Human Rights in Nigeria." *African Human Rights Law Journal* 2, available at SSRN: http://ssrn.com/abstract=1342668 (2008); "A return to the manifest justice principle: a critical examination of the 'reasonable suspicion/apprehension of bias' and 'real possibility of bias' tests for judicial bias in South Africa and England."

Potchefstroom Electronic Law Journal, 12(1) (2009); "The public interest in Namibian copyright law". *Namibian Law Journal* 1: 57–80 (2009).

Haitam SULEIMAN is an Arab Israeli, born in Nazareth. In 2009 he was awarded his PhD by Anglia Ruskin University for a dissertation entitled *Reviving the Waqf in Palestine/Israel*. He undertook field work in Israel/Palestine in 2008-2009.

WANG QILIANG is an associate professor in the Faculty of Law, University of Yunnan, China. Born in Mengzi, Yunnan, China (1977), he was received a Ph.D in the field of Jurisprudence from Yunnan University. He has worked on fieldwork studies in ethnic areas of China since 1995. His recent research has been primarily concerned with legal sociology, legal anthropology and social problems in contemporary China. He is now also a research fellow in the Center of Rural Governance study, Huanzhong University of Science and Technology.

Gordon R. WOODMAN is editor-in-chief of the *Journal of Legal Pluralism.* See further the section 'About the Contributors' in nr. 58 of the *Journal of Legal Pluralism*.

RELIGION, LEGAL PLURALISM AND ORDER IN A MULTIETHNIC SOCIETY: A LEGAL-ANTHROPOLOGICAL STUDY IN CONTEMPORARY CHINA[1]

Wang Qiliang

I. Question and Methodology

> Religion is sociologically interesting not because, as vulgar positivism would have it, it describes the social order ..., but because, like environment, political power, wealth, jural obligation, personal affection, and a sense of beauty, it shapes it. (Gertz 1993: 119)

Actually, the function of religion in 'shaping social order' also gets the attention of legal researchers. In legal study, religion refers to "belief and belief group" (Luo Li 2005: 58). And, more important, "law may exist in religion"(Rüthers 2008). If in thus defining 'law' we go beyond strict law-centered positivism, we would say that religion itself is law, or religion could make law.[2] Therefore, for any society

[1] This research is sponsored by the National Social Science Foundation of China (NSSFC) and the Project of Mainstay Teachers Training of Yunnan University. The author offers grateful acknowledgement.

[2] According to the legal history of China by Liang Zhiping, religious folk law was an element in legal pluralism in ancient China (Liang Zhiping 2003).

in which religion is separated from politics or in which plural religions exist, religion inevitably generates legal pluralism. (On legal pluralism generally, see Merry 1988.)

As a country that carries out a strict separation of religion from politics, China acknowledges and protects in state law the civil freedom of religious belief (People's Daily (China) Commentator 2004). However, the values and doctrines of religion have no place in the formal legal systems of the state. Thus, a discussion on how religion influences law and how this causes legal pluralism in China, must focus on the observation of the basic level in society. This essay will explore certain aspects of the interactions between religion, the state law and the other social controls in grass-roots society. The materials used come from anthropological investigations in grass-roots society in China.

Religions in China are primarily the "Five Main Religions", namely Christianity, Catholicism,[3] Buddhism, Islam and Chinese Taoism. There are over 100m believers, 3,000 religious organizations, and 300,000 clergy in the country (Bureau of State Department 2000). However, in reality, as China is a multiethnic society, the picture of religions is more complicated. On the one hand, we can find various followers of the Five Main Religions in all 56 ethnic groups of China. On the other hand, the Han People (who comprise the largest ethnic group) have a traditional folk religion (Zhou Xing 1998) and the other 55 minorities usually have their own ethnic or primitive religions except for those who belong to the Islamic faith (Yang Xuezheng 1991). Furthermore, the Five Main Religions have experienced the process of localization to different degrees in different areas of China. Every religion necessarily developed certain connections and interaction with local ethnic religions and folk custom, which has caused the Five Main Religions to develop local characteristics (Mou Zhongjian 2005: 7-10). Accordingly, the diverse situations of religion in China have made discussion of the relationship between religion and the state law more intricate.

This essay aims, with the perspective of legal anthropology, to examine the reality of legal pluralism caused by religion in dynamic relations, based on specific cases and ethnographic materials; and to discuss how religion, as one form of social

[3] In China it is usual to use the word "Christianity" to refer to Protestant Christianity, and to refer to Catholic Christianity as Catholicism. That terminology is retained here since it is used in numerous reports and other documents which are relied upon.

control, shapes or influences the formation of social order, and how it plays a role in the legal practice of China against the background of legal pluralism. The essay will also consider whether the legal pluralism generated by religion will destroy or complicate the process of legal unification in China.

II. Religion as Social Control

Religion and the formation of local legal culture

It will be helpful to understand the basic function of religion for human life before we discuss how religion can shape or influence the formation of local legal culture. According to R. Keesing:

> Humans not only weave intricate webs of custom that regulate and order their social lives. They also spin out wider designs of the universe, the forces that govern it, and their place in it. Religious beliefs and rituals are basic in these designs. (Keesing 1976: 385)

In this sense, religion brings a way for its followers to know, to understand and to grasp the world.

As we know, the core issue of law is to make people live and behave in a correct and just manner. However, "what should be 'correct' or 'just' is decided by people's belief or Weltanschauung"(Rüthers 2008). Religion, with its functions in cognition and interpretation, is able to provide its followers some appropriate attitudes to facing nature, society and the other, which generates the correct and just style of living and behavior. In other words, religion defines what are the sacred/mundane, correct/wrong, legitimate/illegal, just/unjust, etc. Given that a legal culture can be regarded as a kind of tendency for human beings, in the course of arranging a social order, to ponder over what should be correct and just, religion then acts as a decisive factor in the formation of this tendency. Religion, hence, could be a basic element in forming local legal culture. Certainly, the extent to which religion can influence the formation of local legal culture depends on the status of religion in people's life, since human beings also grasp other methods (such as art, theory and science) to understand the world (Niu Shulin 2005: 135-41). In the village of the *Hui* people in Yunnan, China, where Islam deeply affects the social life and the spirit world of believers, religion plays a dominant role in the formation of local legal culture. For example, the family education of the *Hui* people includes 'faith', 'conduct' and 'living skill', which link closely to Islam. Especially education in 'conduct', which guides people's lives and requires them to behave in correct and just manner, acquires its standards directly from the Koran (Na Qi 2001: 172-74). This kind of standard of conduct thus composes the core of local legal culture.

In general, religion's contribution to the construction of the social order of grass-roots society and to the formation of the pattern of legal pluralism lies mainly in the fact that religion can create a certain religious legal culture which dominates every aspect of religious social control. More important, as religious social control has developed into a part of local social control, religious legal culture also has an important influence on the formation of local legal culture. According to the diversity of both ethnicity and religion, however, the local legal culture shaped by religion bears a plural characteristic: on the one hand, different religions create different religious legal cultures; on the other hand, even the same religion can generate distinctive legal cultures with reference to different places or ethnic groups. In this sense, people can arrange social order in terms of different patterns.

Religion and the formation of local norms

As mentioned above, the conduct tendency (preference) that religion provides in the formation of local legal culture can also produce corresponding specific norms which guide, encourage or restrict people's behavior. Religion would, at least, promote or influence the formation of two sorts of local norms: one is the rule with the function of maintaining the religious doctrine, ceremony, organization and purity of belief in the community, the other is the rule for daily life.

(a) Norms relevant to religion

The reason why we discuss religion together with law and social order is that "religion is one kind of social activity" (Liang Hongfei 2003: 138). Religion involves the ways of thinking and living of a community. In order to safeguard the doctrine held by the religious community, to perform the religious ritual process, to guarantee the purity of the religion, a set of norms has been produced from within the community.

The following is a case from my fieldwork in *Mann village* of the Dai People. *Mann village* has faith in both Hinayana (a branch of Buddhism) and traditional ethnic religion. On the one hand, some local norms are generated based on Hinayana doctrine:

> *Norms of conduct in the temple*: (1) Male must take off shoes outside the hall of *Mian* temple; (2) Female must take off both shoes and socks at the gate of *Mian* temple; (3) Seculars cannot die in the temple.
>
> *Norms of maintenance of monks and temples*: The maintenance of the *Mian* Temples and the living expenses of monks are dependent on money collected from villagers. In addition to multiple "Offerings to the Buddha" by villagers consisting of money and material for maintenance and sustenance, there are offerings of food by villagers, who are divided into groups according to which Villagers Commission they belong to. In Village Mann, once a monk decides to devote himself to the Buddha, his livelihood, from his youth to old age, through illness, to death, will be paid for by money donated by villagers.
>
> *Norms for behaviour of monks*: (1) The "Ten Commandments", prescribing no killing, no stealing, no communications with girls (including not being in love with girls, not entertaining girls), no lies, no drinking, no lunch after noon, no gambling, no make-up, no dressing in clothes with long sleeves or wearing of high-heeled shoes, no wearing of watches, bracelets or necklaces. (2) Loss of any of the temple's possessions will be paid for by Buddhist monks. (3) No interference in village business. (4) A monk is not allowed to die in his home. Otherwise, his parents must invite monks to dispel demons, and pay the fees. (5) Monks should not sleep overnight at home.
>
> *Norms for ordinary villagers toward monks*: (1) No touching of a monk's head. (2) Parents are not allowed to beat or criticize a son who is monk. When it is really necessary for parents to punish a son who is a monk, they must wrap the stick with

> yellow clothes and then beat him.

On the other hand, some local norms come from the traditional ethnic religion of the *Dai* people.

> *Maintenance of the symbol and ceremony of sacredness*: (1) The wood in the Village Centre is not allowed to be touched. (2) The Protection of the Village Center is paid for with money contributed by the villagers at the rate of RMB 100 every year, to cover the activities and repair of Zhao Mann. (3) In the ceremony of *Nin Mann* (meaning sacrifices to the god of the village), no members of other villages are allowed to enter the village. During the ceremony, the village is cordoned off by bamboo leaves and grass barring the gate. An intruder will have to pay RMB 15, and give a pack of glutinous rice and two wax sticks to the god of the village as punishment, for the purpose of getting forgiveness.

In the *Mann* village, some regulations dealing with the relationship between the two kinds of religions cited above also arise since they interweave in the villagers' social and spiritual world. For example, leaders in Buddhism and the main figures of local primitive religion are well distinguished and also cooperate.

(b) Norms relevant to daily life

Religion, as a way to cognizing and interpreting the world, becomes a resource pool of information for its followers. People use this resource to react to incidents and phenomenon, and to direct their behavior. These directions will penetrate into people's daily life and become norms in daily life. Here I will discuss the case from my fieldwork in *Mann* village of the *Dai* People.

> *Norms of family life*: (1) when building a house, both a front and a back door are necessary so that the soul of ancestors can come home. (2) Never put firewood in front of the slate tripod, and only elderly men can sit there. (3) Others may not enter the host's bedroom. (4) The domestic house should have two poles, a "princess pillar" and a "prince pillar", where ancestors' souls live. People may not turn their backs on them due to their sacred

meaning. (5) The ceremony of "live in new house" (the couple's new house) must be carried out before 12:00 noon. (6) The body of a deceased must not go to cremation before 12:00 noon (the moon taboo being an exception). If the people 'die badly' (meaning by an accident), they must go to cremation on the same day. If they die well, their body can stay for one more day before cremation. And these two kinds of cremations take place in different 'Ann forests'.

Norms of village public life: (1) Villagers may not work or go to other villages until a cremation is completed. It is *Zhaoman* who will take the responsibility for settling any dispute occurring as a result of a breach of this rule. (*Zhaoman* is regarded as the head of the village, his authority being derived from primitive religion.) (2) When a person in a village dies, people from other villages cannot enter this village until the cremation of the body is completed. When somebody violates this rule and affronts God, *Zhaoman* will punish him by requiring him to pay 15 yuan, a chicken, 10 packets of glutinous rice and two pieces of wax to offer a sacrifice to God. (3) The people of another village may not pull firewood through this village. It is considered to 'burn people' (cremate them). *Zhaoma*n will punish an offender by requiring him to give 1 jin oil, 1 jin rice and two pieces of wax to offer a sacrifice to God. (4) In a year when too many people in other villages die, villagers from those villages may not enter this village lest they affront God. Otherwise *Zhaoman* will punish them at his discretion.

Norms concerning the purchase of livestock and going outside the village: (1) When the villagers buy livestock or poultry, *Zhaoman* will determine whether it has diseases. Then *Zhaoman* will tell God and pray for safety. Only then can villagers breed from them. (2) When the villagers go outside the village, they pray for God's protection.

Norms on reproduction: (1) A married woman cannot return to her mother's home to give birth. (2) When a pregnant women dies, the fetus must be removed through matrix and be minced. Then the mother and the fetus respectively are cremated. (3)

> During the month after giving birth, a mother may not pass out of the door or enter other people's homes. If she has to, she must take a sickle with her on her waist. (4) If a baby dies before it is half a year old, it must be thrown in the river and drift away downstream.
>
> *Taboo on the moon*: (1) During a lunar eclipse villagers set off firecrackers. If you have a pillar, you must hit it with a sword or water it with wine. (2) During full Moon, when you drink, you must save some wine to water the pillar at the time of the lunar eclipse. (3) If a couple are at a girl's home during a lunar eclipse and she is at home, her parents will ask them to stay there for the night. That means they are married. (4) When somebody dies during Full Moon on January 15, they should immediately hold the funeral. (5) If somebody dies at home during a lunar eclipse, his body cannot be taken out through the door. The family must break the roof and pass the body through the hole and then down to the ground. If the body has edema, it must go to cremation at once. (6) From July 15 (the date of the closing door ceremony) to October 15(the date of the opening door ceremony), activities such as lovemaking, building new houses and moving to a new house are forbidden.

In the *Mann* village, religion holds a crucial position in people's spiritual world. Religion has not only produced norms in relation to religious doctrine, articles of creed, sacred places, ceremonies and religious authority, but has also produced norms to regulate people's daily life. The quantity, scale and range of this kind of local norms, however, are decided by the actual status of religion in people's life, which differ between different villages and communities. Generally, the religions which have been highly rationalized, such as Christianity, or Catholicism, generate fewer daily norms than the ethnic traditional ones. Nevertheless, there is no doubt that religion always produces some local norms, more or fewer, in the grass-roots society.

Religion and the emergence of local social control

Religion's influence on the social order could also be attributed to its "nature of organization" (Liang Hongfei 2003: 139). Every religion has a certain organization, no matter what may be its developmental stage. Some have a high level of organization, but others may just have some persons temporarily in charge and loose organization. There must be some religious authority, no matter what the organization of the religion. Other than a simple faith organization or a mere guide to belief, religious groups and their authority figures always become local social controllers and take responsibility for realizing the social function of religion.

To what extent this kind of social controller can play its roles, and how it gets along with other kinds of social controllers, are determined by different factors, such as its scope of influence and the number of believers. For example, in a village of *Lahu* People, the authority figures from both Hinayana and primitive religion have all become key persons in the administration of the local village. They are mainly in charge of implementing rules and settling disputes, and act as social controllers in keeping village order (Wang Xiaozhu 2000 112-53). In another case of a *Hani* village, "*Migu*", the authority in the traditional religion of the *Hani* people, takes responsibility for arranging local religious activities and ensuring the observance of many norms about daily life (He Siqiang 2000: 219-30). Even highly rationalized religions will usually expand their functions and become powers of social control once they enter a village, So, for example, in a village where Christianity is widespread, the follower's behaviour is regulated by religious norms. A clergyman takes charge of admonishing persons who violate relgious law and has the right to expel a person from the Church (Xiao Ying 2000: 229). Another case shows that the believers in Christianity in *Zala* village need to get permission from the priest of local church before getting married (Zhao Mei 2000: 105).

Religion and the settlement of disputes

As a kind of social control, religion itself can develop the means to settle disputes or to influence the process of settlements. Parties in a dispute may turn to God or faith to resolve their problems if both parties share the same belief and one trusts the genuineness of the other's religious belief. A very typical case is the submission to various forms of God's judgment to settle disputes in some societies (Deng Minwen 1991). It is not true that God's judgments have disappeared from out lives. Even today, the *Yi* people community in *Liangshan* of China still uses the method of taking an oath to settle disputes. Some religious rites are conducted for the person who claims to be innocent. In the rite the person is required to recite words of an oath invoking the *pneuma* of the ancestors, swearing that he/she will die just like an ox, goat or chicken if he/she told a lie, and then killing an ox, goat or chicken. To swear on one's own life is regarded as unlucky but is enough to testify to one's innocence so that the opposite party believes them. (See Qumuyuzhi and Liu Yaohan 1998: 39-41. Also see Zhang Yonghe 2006, arguing that the reason why norms such as swearing oaths can play roles in social control is always that these norms exist in the specific belief system.) Swearing becomes an effective way to settle disputes because of the worship of the ancestors of the *Yi* people. The people believe that the *pneuma* of ancestors can control all disasters and blessings on earth and also can be the judge of the person taking the oath.

Though religion itself can be the origin of disputes, it also can provide particular means to promote the settlement of disputes. For example, there is a customary norm in *Mann* village, where I did fieldwork, and the nearby villages of the *Dai* people, according to which, if a person of A village has died, the people of A village should not enter other villages until the cremation of the deceased has been completed. This customary norm originated from religious belief. Case 1 below demonstrates how a dispute was caused because of a violation of this customary norm between *Mann* village and a nearby village in 2000 and how it was finally settled successfully by the religious customary law (Wang Qiliang 2004).

Case 1: the incident in which Yan offended Duan village

On the early morning of January 20, 2000, an elder of *Mann* village died and the village head broadcast the news within the village. The family members of the deceased hurried to inform their relatives. *Yan*, the grandson-in-law of the deceased, was on his way to deliver a message to *Menhun* village, 20 kilometers from *Mann* village, by motorcycle. Having no driving license, to avoid a police check *Yan* made a detour and passed through *Duan* village. The villagers of *Duan* village blocked the way and were ready to amerce *Yan* 12 yuan. However, *Yan* fled, which angered the villagers of *Duan* village. As a result, the incident became a dispute between the two villages and *Duan* village demanded that *Mann* village pay a penalty of 500 yuan. Thereupon, the head of *Mann* village called in *Yan*, *Zhaoman, Buzhang* (the supervisor of the Buddhist monks in the local Mian temple and also the village magician), cadres of the Villagers' Committee, and some CCP members, and conducted a negotiation with *Duan* village with lasted over two hours. On the failure to reach agreement, *Mann* village then brought a counterclaim: if the deceased of *Duan* village was to be buried in the "Dragon

Forest" (the common graveyard shared by *Mann, Duan* and *Man'e*n villages), which was located exactly on the boundary of *Mann* village, a charge of 1,000 yuan would be levied by *Mann* village. Furthermore, if a *Duan* villager entered Mann village to deliver a message to relatives, *Mann* village would fine that person 1,000 yuan. These propositions worked and both parties finally went back the customary rule: *Duan* village punished *Yan* with a fine of 15 yuan, a chicken, 10 packets of glutinous rice, and two candles to offer sacrifice to the god of village.

In this case the dispute was caused by the breach of a customary norm based on the traditional ethnic religion. It is religion that links the separated items - the death of a non-native villager, prohibition on entering a village, *Zhaoman,* a fine, a chicken, the offering of a sacrifice to the god of a village, and Dragon Forest - and forms a coherent system which both creates norms and also generates disputes. The rule of not entering a village is closely related to the local knowledge and imagination. In the ethnic religion of the *Dai* People, if non-native villagers enter a village before the deceased of another village has been buried, the native god of this village will be insulted and the native villagers will lose the protection of the god. So the punishment of 15 yuan, a chicken, 10 packets of glutinous rice, and two candles is to pray for the renewal of god's blessing on this village. Viewing this case, it is found that both the occurrence and the settlement of a dispute are processes full of local characteristics in which religious customary rules and religious authority have strong influence.

Even those religions which lack designated clergymen and systematic doctrines can work in the settlement of disputes. In the folk belief of the *Han* people, the memorial tablet of an ancestor is regarded as the symbol of the *pneuma* of that ancestor, and bears the social meanings of a comforting emotion and mentality, of the settling of disputes among family members, and of the affirmation of identity recognition (Li Yiyuan 1997: 279). The memorial tablet of ancestor has been used as a legitimate symbol of status and identity in dispute settlement. Accordingly, religion can have an influence on the settlement of disputes in various ways.

Religious social control and legal pluralism

To sum up, religion has been making or influencing the formation of local legal culture, creating various norms, producing social control, and playing roles in dispute settlement. The interaction among these four aspects causes religion to have a function of producing general social control. How can religion work in these four aspects? What kind of effectiveness does religion have in constructing, keeping and affecting social order? The answers to these questions will depend on the status of religion in the community, its influence in people's spiritual world and its permeability in daily life. That is why religion could act as a key factor in keeping social order in some villages (Hou Junsheng and Tan Jianghua 2004), but would have less effect in other villages (Feng Liangfang 2000). There is no doubt, however, that religion will always have some influence on the social order if only religious belief exists (Zhang Xiaohui and Wang Qiliang 2005) And more important, the coexistence of religious social control and the other social controls will create patterns of legal pluralism whose complexity in a certain society will be determined by a balancing of all forces of various social controls. In this sense, religion has become a necessary factor in the discussion of the construction of legal systems in China.

III. Encounter of Plural Laws

Religious social control and other unofficial social controls

Unofficial norms, such as rules in the family, taboos in the community, and regulations in a social group, are ubiquitous in social life at a basic level (Wang Qiliang 2006). Thus numerous interactions will necessarily occur between religious social control and the other unofficial social controls.

The first such situation appears in a community where people keep to traditional ethnic religion alone. Given that the culture of the village has never been broken down, or it has been restored after a breakdown, religion itself will naturally and usually interweave with folk life. Religious social control, as a result, may develop a high level of integration with the other unofficial social controls, and this will give positive support to the actual social order. (See also: Yao Jide 2000; He Siqiang 2000; Zhang Xiaohui 2000.) If, however, the local culture has been broken down, both religious social control and the other unofficial social controls way as a necessary consequence decline within the cultural system. In this circumstance, religious social control may fail to well integrate with the other social controls and the different controls may fail to develop a stable relationship between each other. This can easily cause social conflicts in some sense (Wang Qiliang 2001).

The second situation, occurring in a community where plural religious beliefs spread widely, would be more complicated. On the one hand, some obvious cases from the ethnic villages in Yunnan, China, where people believe in both Hinayana and traditional ethnic religion, demonstrate that, by experiencing a long period of interaction, plural religions have actually developed certain inter-recognition and some harmonious relationship (Zhang Xiaohui 2000; Wang Xiaozhu 2000; Tan Xiaojian 2000). In this case, conflicts among different religions rarely happen, and a set of rules for settling conflicts could be found even if it did happen. In the meantime, a general religious social control generated from plural religions could have a high level of integration with other unofficial social controls. On the other hand, the situation in which traditional ethnic religion exists with Christianity or Catholicism becomes complex. In the case of *Dengga village* of the *Jingpo* people, who believe in traditional ethnic religion, Christianity and Catholicism, plural religious social controls keep a balance between each other and accord with folk life, so that social conflicts are seldom caused (Wang Jiao 2000: 224-27). However, in the case of *Zhala* village of the *Nu* people, where Christianity, Catholicism, Lamaism and traditional ethnic religion all exist, differences between the regulations and doctrines of the various religions have caused some problems. For example, controversies have occurred among family members whose beliefs differ; Lamaist has looked down upon Catholic; Christians have been forbidden to engage in ethnic dancing which is a traditional form of communication in the village (Zhao Mei 2000). These problems, although they do not yet extend to the point of endangering the stability of the village order, show that plural religious social controls may fail to keep a balance and to form a favorable integration with folk life. Generally speaking, in a society where plural religions exist, the relationship among different religious social controls depends on the extent to which the religions can tolerate each other and also on the existence of a single effective negotiating mechanism between the religions.

Based on the ethnographic materials, it can be said that the complex relations between religious social control and other unofficial social controls vary according to the specific situation of each village.

Religious social control and the implementation of state law

In contemporary China, it is difficult to find an area where state law has no influence at all, even in remote ethnic border districts. Therefore, religious social control, as one kind of unofficial social control, has also interacted with state law. To examine the connection between religious social control and state law, the paper will discuss how religion affects the implementation of state law in the following three ways.

(a) Religion as a support to state law

Whether state law can be put into effect successfully does not simply depend on the mandatory force of the government. Beyond the limited power and administrative resources which the government has at its disposal, a large number of laws seek support from local society to achieve their goals. In the multiethnic and multi-religious society of China, religion, as a social control, holds an important position in maintaining the stability of the social order. In some sense, to return to religion for support means to acquire support from secular society. Many ethnographic materials reveal that religion usually plays a positive role in advancing the implementation of law and sustaining social order in most communities.[4] However, such a positive effect may be directly or indirectly linked to each specific situation.

On the one hand, religion, as a social control power sustaining or producing a micro social order, may have the capacity to create a certain order which law will recognize or pursue. Then state law, with the help of religion, can achieve its goal of keeping social stability without using mandatory measures. This is the universal situation in which religion implicitly supports law. In the case of the village of the *Hui* people, numerous religious regulations regarding people's morality and conduct are consistent with the requirements of law, so that the cost of legal implementation becomes low (Na Qi 2001: 197-211). We also find that many religious disciplines, for example those of Christianity, Catholicism and Buddhism, are in accord with the goal of implementation of law (Lv Zhaoyi and Hong Mei 2004; Xiao Ying 2000). Religious social control in some villages has even developed, with the emergence of new social problems, to cope with social crimes and problems by coordinating with the secular norms of the village and with state law. For example, in a village of the *A'chang* people, taking or

[4] This is shown, for example, by a series of ethnographic materials generated from two large-scale investigations in ethnic villages of China by Yunnan University in 2000 and 2003. These produced 55 ethnographies for 55 ethnic minorities in China.

trafficking in drugs is forbidden by religious norms (Wang Zhiliang 2000).

On the other hand, religion can also respond to state law in an explicitly positive way. This kind of contribution usually relies on a religious authority. As the interpreter of religious doctrine and the guide to followers with respect to their conduct, the religious authority frequently obtains high respect from the government in China (e.g. GUANGXI CPPCC Review Group 2002, a report on an investigation in Hainan Province). Local government often inclines to seek support from such authorities in dealing with affairs relevant to religion, including the implementation of law and dispute settlement. For example, in the Tibet Area of Qinghai Province, China, if in a case of homicide judgment in a judicial procedure has failed to settle the dispute between the two parties, the religious authority may step in to mediate (Zhang Gimin 1993: 202-32). Another case from ethnographic material also illustrates that, in a village of the *Bao'an* people, who believe in Islam, local government has to seek help from the Imam of the local mosque to carry out the regulations for marriage registration (Du Xian and Peng Qingshen 2004: 105).

(b) Legal conflict and legal failure resulting from religion

Religion, however, still holds its own value and controlling style. The differences between this form of social control and legal rationality inevitably produce conflicts between religion and state law in certain circumstances, which can lead to high costs in implementation of state law or even to its failure.

The following case indicates a sharp conflict between religious social control and state policy. Family planning work in *Stone po* village began in 1983. The *Sala* people there, who believe in Islam, consider family planning an unreasonable thing. According to their canon, for a woman over four months pregnant to have an abortion can be regarded as serious as committing murder. It is very difficult for the local women to follow the administrative regulations. This kind of religious belief has played a negative role in attempts to carry out family planning policy (Zhu Heshuang and Xie Zuo 2004: 103).

In this case, family planning policy has met with social resistance because of the huge differences existing in religious norms and the official system. Although family planning policy is implemented ultimately with mandatory force, the local government is subject to high costs as a result (Zhu Heshuang and Xie Zuo 2004:

103). In another case from my fieldwork in a village of the *Dai* people, religious social control caused the local villagers to expel a person who was regarded as \ 'Pipa Ghost', an act which violated the criminal law (Wang Qiliang 2004: 100-1). The case is described below.

Case 2: the 'Pipa Ghost'

An old woman of *Mann* village who had long been a widow was regarded as a 'Pipa Ghost'. According to local rumor that she could call up monsters and had harmed many people in the nearby villages. In 1998, a person of a nearby village fell ill and died. This incident led dozens of villagers to enter *Mann* village, destroy the house of the 'Pipa Ghost', and injure the old woman. The local villagers of *Mann* did not stop the neighbors, and indeed thought the 'Pipa Ghost' deserved a worse fate. Finally, the cadre of Mann village had to build a simple bamboo room for the woman in a roadside bamboo forest outside the village. Thereafter the 80-year-old woman had an isolated life.

A similar incident happened in 2002 when I did my last fieldwork in *Mann* village. The people of a neighboring village expelled a 'Pipa Ghost' and her husband, and strongly opposed any proposal that they could come back. Ultimately, the local government of the township had to arrange for the couple to become caretakers of a reservoir far away from the village.

This kind of conflict also occurred in a case from my fieldwork in which certain religious customs of the *Hani* people made villagers violate the provisions of the Forest Protection Law (Wang Qiliang 2004: 100-1).

The cases mentioned can be classed as instances of 'open' resistance to state law or policy caused by religion. However, religion can also result in the failure of law in an indirect way. For example, in some villages, the canons of Christianity or Catholicism forbid follower to marry pagans (Zheng Weichuan 2000: 255-56). These constrain people's freedom of religious belief and freedom of marriage indirectly. To some extent, such restrictions have reduced the effectiveness of law in protecting the civic rights of freedom of belief freedom and of marriage.

Nevertheless, religions which have been diffused widely and which have developed well in villages for long periods, such as the traditional ethnic religions, primitive religions or Christianity, Catholicism and Buddhism, are less likely to have conflicts with state law. In contrast to newly developed or undercover religions conflicts between the former and state law are partial or minor as those religions have historically experienced the process of integrating with politics and social life. Conflict between the latter and state law can have more serious consequences, given that the latter are less well developed in their religious doctrines and are highly secret (Deng Fei 2006; Liu Zhiming and Deng Fei 2006a, 2006b).

(c) Transformation of religious social control rooted in law

The case described below argues that the relationship between religious social control and state institutions is not a simple relation of complementarity or confrontation. The state institution also can reshape and influence religious social control.

Case 3 Temple education or school education?

According to the custom of *Mann* village and other nearby *Dai* villages, boys around the age of seven should become boy *bonzes* in the local temples, where they will learn Sutra and the *Dai* language. In general, the historical transmission and development of the *Dai* language and culture is attributed mainly to temple education, as temples acted as essential loci for religious and ethnic cultural activities before the emergence of state-run schools. However, the age for becoming a *bonze* is the same as the school starting age for children under the compulsory education system in China. To solve the conflict between national education and temple education, the government of *Meng* township used to set up special '*bonze* classes' in schools, where students learnt both Chinese and the *Dai* language, in order to ensure that boy *bonzes* could receive formal education at school. The schools also tried their best to satisfy the *bonzes*' special study and living needs, and some boy *bonzes* went to these schools at that time. However, the results of the measures were far from satisfactory. The enrolment rate of boys of school-going age at the *Mann* village school was 98% in 1998, but the rate was not sustained since there was a high drop-out rate for *bonze* students. At the same time, educational facilities in *Dai* temples became better, with for example televisions and DVDs becoming available, and these distracted boy *bonzes* from school. Even if they did not leave school, it was common for them to skip classes. Because of the special status of boy *bonzes* in *Dai* areas, parents could not discipline their own *bonze* children and teachers in schools could not punish *bonze* students. Thus it was difficult to get the boys to receive formal full-time education once they became boy *bonzes*.

People in the *Mann* village took different attitudes towards the issue of whether boys should become *bonzes*. Some elders argued that boys should become *bonzes* so as to receive temple education, which they thought was better than school education. Many middle-aged parents had no preference between the two, but let their children become *bonzes* as that was 'what other parents do'. Parents were also afraid of being thought poor if they did not send their children to the temple, as the cost of becoming a *bonze* was several thousand yuan. A minority of villagers, however, insisted that becoming a *bonze* was not good for a child's formal education, because the child became slack and lazy once he became a *bonze*. One of the villagers who had a daughter of 14 years and a son of 11, for example, had his son removed from his religious status one year after the boy became a *bonze* to ensure that he received a good school education and higher education for the sake of his future.

From the year 2000, the government of the township in which the *Dai* village lies began to enforce strictly the *Measures of Implementation of Compulsory Education in Meng Township (Provisional), 1999*. The rules provide:

> Religion is not allowed to interfere with school education. Those temples which accept students of school attendance age to become *bonzes*, along with the student's guardian and head of the village are subject to a penalty of RMB 3000-5000 respectively.

The rules guarantee that among the *Dai* people boys can only become *bonzes* after finishing their compulsory education. When the author went back to the *Mann* village in 2001, there were no boy *bonzes* in the temples, as all boys of the appropriate age went to school. As a result, the village has had to 'borrow' three boy *bonzes* from the neighboring village.

Setting aside the question whether the measures enacted by the *Meng* township government were appropriate or not, it can be seen clearly that the official practice in law implementation has aimed to transform a certain aspect of religious social control, that is, the time at which a boy might enter the temple and become a *bonze*. The measure proved to be effective in the end. From the case we can see that, if some effort is made in terms of state law (including legal implementation), there exists a possibility to regulate and integrate religion into state law. In other words, religion as a type of social control can be transformed towards the target set by the law, through the law's influence.

IV. Conclusion: Religion, Social Harmony and Legal Unity under Legal Pluralism in China

To sum up, religious social control objectively intensifies the character of legal pluralism. However, does it therefore present a challenge to social harmony and legal unity? To answer this question, we have to make clear first that religion, as an essential part of the explanation of the ultimate meaning of human life, will continue to exist as a universal social cultural phenomenon in long term. Therefore, state law should choose a realistic attitude in dealing with matters related to religion.

As mentioned above, some conflicts between religious social control and other social controls (including state law) are inevitable. However, these conflicts may also be resolvable. In practice, in those highly rationalized religions which have attained the "highest reaches of philosophical sophistication" (Geertz 1993: 174-175) the rules and norms of religion seldom get directly involved with the secular life. Those traditional ethnic religions which have greatly permeated mundane life and which regulate daily life in obvious ways on the other hand also keep the "means-ends" feature. The factor of superstition or witchcraft in the ethnic religions usually finds its cause in the realities of that life or has direct links with the difficult situations in which people find themselves (Lu Qun 2006). In the absence of these practical conditions superstition or witchcraft would lose its base of existence. The case of 'Pipa Ghost' cited above is a good example.

I was puzzled by the incidents of the expulsion of 'Pipa Ghost' in *Mann* village and other *Dai* people's villages in Xishuangbanna, Yunnan. Geenrally the friendly and kindly characters of these people and the profound *Dai* culture have always impressed me deeply during my fieldwork. I was shocked by their merciless and cruel behavior in expelling 'Pipa Ghost'. This kind of contradiction forced me to seek deep reasons. The expulsion of the 'Pipa Ghost' is closely related to ethnic religious belief. The *Dai* people in *Mann* village believe in the common existence of ghosts and gods and hold that seven main kinds of ghosts exist in their living world: Piya, Pipa, Piga, Pishe, Pihong, Piwang, and Pimeng. Of these the Pipa ghost is the hardest to expel. Buzhang of *Mann* village admitted that he was able to expel the other four ghosts, but not Piya, Pipa and Piga. Firmly holding this faith in ethnic religion, *Dai* people naturally consider that people who become Pipa ghosts cease to be human beings. Actions such as isolating them, damaging their property, and causing them physical harm are therefore just parts of the ceremony of expelling a ghost in this specific cultural logic. According to the system of classification in *Dai* culture, the person declared to be a Pipa ghost has been placed in the category of 'ghost', and to treat ghosts in a merciless and cruel way in not in any way inhuman. For *Dai* people, expelling a Pipa ghost successfully means the victory of justice against evil, according to a 'natural rule'. From this point of view, the conduct of expelling a Pipa ghost has a reasonable basis in the cultural premises of the *Dai* people.

More important, this paper argues that the view of humans as clearly differented from ghosts is deeply rooted in specific social reasons. My further research shows that the reclassification of some humans as ghosts is directly linked to difficult situations that the local villagers face in real life.

According to the recollection of Mr. Wang Lianfang, an experienced researcher on racial problems in China:

> Expelling 'the Pipa Ghost' is a method of expelling diseases in Dai minority regions. ... the Pipa Ghost seems to be a natural disaster but is in fact a man-made calamity. Since medical groups have entered ethnic areas, they have met many incidents of expelling Pipa Ghosts. The members of medical groups had to take every opportunity to persuade the people, while at the same time they gave patients medical treatment till they recovered. Then the news spread fast that the Communist Party could cure those who were bitten by the Pipa Ghosts. Even some people who used to turn to Buddhism to cure their diseases came to us for medical treatment. The film Moyadai, which was shot in the 1960s, was a true reflection of these cases. (Wang Lianfang 1998)

In fact, the expulsion of the Pipa Ghost usually happened when patients failed to get effective medical treatment. This action, as a type of exorcism, performs the function of relieving both the worries of the sick and the panic of local people, and confirms the fact that everything in life is still under control. In other words, the act of expelling the Pipa Ghost originates from lack of knowledge of illness and medical treatment, and is a method of dealing with this problem of living and life. Consequently, the expulsion of ghosts was popular among minorities like the *Dai* before medical treatment networks were built up in 1960s[5] and it has happened less and less since the improvement of medical facilities. However, in the last two decades incidents of expelling Pipa Ghost have resumed in some minority villages where medical facilities were in extremely short supply. This kind of phenomenon illustrates exactly that people have clear idea of when to seek help from witchcraft and when to abandon it (Liang Yongjia and Lee Shaomin 2002: 340-67. For discussion of public health situation in ethnic minorities areas also see: Wang Qiliang et al. 2003).

If the instance of the expulsion of Pipa ghost can be understood in terms of the inherent system of religious culture, it is possible to see some functional reasons for interpreting such 'illegal' or 'unreasonable' religious norms in terms of human rights. This gives clues as to ways to reduce the negative elements in religious belief and to prevent the violation of law. In the case of Pipa ghost, improving medical treatment could be a good starting-point.[6]

It is the element of superstition and witchcraft in ethnic religion that might generate conflict with state law, since such religious ideas provide problematic guides to understanding the world. In other words, legal conflict caused by religion originates from 'ideas' which could be changed in some reasonable way. Therefore, to avoid or resolve conflicts between religion and law, we should first examine whether there are any serious defects in the administrative systems of

[5] A similar example is the disease of smallpox. The medical preservative and treatment for smallpox was unavailable in the ethnic minorities areas of Yunnan Province, China, during 1950s and '60s. Failing to find any scientific explanation of this infectious disease, local people regarded it as a phenomenon of ghosts harming humans, to counter which witchcraft became legitimate. However, people abandoned witchcraft after treatment by vaccination had been extended to these areas. ('Fighting against smallpox', a program on this subject presented in the series 'Exploration and Discovery' on CCTV 10 of China, 4 May, 2005.)

[6] In some sense, measures for resolving the problem are determined by how people interpret the specific phenomenon. Since Mr Wang Liangfang and his colleagues of the working group at that time had no particular objective and a pragmatic attitude towards the expulsion, they were likely to fail to discern the fundamental reason for it and so to take appropriate measures against it.

law, rather than merely relying on coercive implementation of law. For example, we need to remember that people will turn to religion, and even to superstition or witchcraft, if they fail to obtain social security and medical treatment from the public health system.

From a broader perspective of development in China, religion does not necessarily threaten legal unity. Harold J. Berman illustrated the close link between law and religion in western society and tried in his research to prove that law and religion shared common elements and features (Berman 1974). What Berman worried about was that the sacredness of law could be lost and the effect of law weakened when religion declined. In that way, law could become a mere scrap of paper as people lost belief in it. However, China differs from both western societies that have experienced the demands of religious conformity, as Berman mentioned, and from countries that believe in Islam (Horn 2006). Religion as social control in China is generally separated from state law. None of the doctrine or ethics of religion is incorporated in legislation. The legality and authority of law have no necessary link with religion. In addition, the experience of plural religions in the society of China contrasts with that of the drive for religious unity in Europe of the Middle Ages. Consequently, the various religions in China do not share doctrines nor have a common advocacy. State law holds greater authority than any other form of social control including those provided by religion. Law protects freedom of religious belief but limits religious activity within the legal regime. In this way, state law can develop its function of construction and integration by regulating religious social control and the other social controls, but this is possible only if law remains neutral among all religions and avoids designating a certain morality or life style as the only legitimate one (Rüthers 2008). It can be proved that in practice religion itself, rather than a static object, has the capacity of developing and perfecting itself in the process of social transformation. In the case of *Sala* village mentioned above, local people are gradually becoming willing to accept family planning policy since the local government has kept propagating its politicies in the village. The people of *Bao'an* village have come to understand the value of marriage registration. Even the conflict between the ethnic customs of the *Hani* people and forest protection has been skilfully resolved.[7] These facts prove

[7] According to customs of the *Hani* people, the coffin for a dead elder should be made from a single mountain osmanthus tree, which cannot then be used for any other deceased. However, the mountain osmanthus tree is one of the valuable species protected by the state, and it can be found only in remote mountains of a Nature Protection Area. Therefore, *Hani* residents living in this area broke state

that, in the practical process of legal operation, religion will not necessarily challenge or destroy the unity of the rule of law, in spite of the existence of differences between religious social control and law.

However, a cautious attitude should be taken in fashioning the legal construction when state law attempts to integrate religious social control. As we know, for most ethnic minorities religion comprises an essential part of ethnic culture and has become a cultural expression of the group (Lv Daji and Zhang Shihui 2004). Religious social control holds a central position in the traditional social order of communities. A sudden or huge breakdown of religious tradition will lead to the discontinuance of the culture and a rupture of social control, which may result in the collapse of social order. China has had such lessons in history (Wang Qiliang 2001). Taking the perspective of legal pluralism, it is necessary to forbid conduct that seriously harms human rights and violates human nature in the name of religion, as has occurred, for example, when some illegal religious organizations appeared in the areas of ethnic minorities (Yin Yonglin 2000). But, generally speaking, it could be better for state law to adops a prudent and tolerant attitude in responding to problems resulting from religion, especially newly rising or illegal religions. Just as the analysis of Li Yiyuan of issues of the localization of religion movement in Taiwan (Li Yiyuan 1997), we have to keep seeking support from various social resources, such as social work, and social policy adjustment, to cope with different social matters which state law fails to resolve completely.

---

laws and regulations every time they cut down a mountain osmanthus tree. In order to protect these trees and also to preserve the *Hani* funeral customs, the Nature Protection Bureaus in Shiswobana have since 1999 recommended *Manalen* village to work with a Nature Protection Fund in a co-operative management programme with the title: 'I am growing with little trees'. Supported by this programme, the village residents provided 60 acres of undeveloped mountain areas and organized students to plant mountain osmanthus tree, each with the planter's own name card on it. If a student dies, the tree the student planted will be used to make the student's coffin. 400 trees planted in 1999 and later survive. The participating students also gained consciousness of need for forest protection. In the longer term, the "I am growing with little trees" programme as a multi-functional activity targets the preservation of traditional ethnic customs, the resolution of the conflict between ethnic customs and forest protection, and the afforestation of remote mountains.

In conclusion, religion, is a double-bladed sword. It could on the one hand become a positive strength for shaping harmonious social order if state law deals with it appropriately. It could on the other hand cause conflicts if state law deals with it partially and unreasonably. A cautious and reasonable way of treating religion has definitely become an important requirement in the process of legal construction in China.

References

(Note: where works have been published only in Chinese, English translations of the titles are given here; where non-Chinese works have been translated into Chinese, details of the Chinese translations are given.)

BERMAN, Harold J.
1974 *The Interaction of Law and Religion.* Nashville TN: Abingdon Press [Translation by Liang Zhiping, 2003. Beijing: Politics and Law University of China Press].
BUREAU OF STATE DEPARTMENT
2000 *Communique of State Department, P.R.C* 10: 21.
DENG FEI
2006 'An Underground religious organization and sixteen homicide cases.' *Phoenix Weekly* 11: 16-23.
DENG MINWEN
1991 *On Gods Judgments*. Guiyang: Guizhou People Press.
DU XIAN and PENG QINGSHEN (eds.)
2004 *Bao'an People: the Investigation of Dadun village of Jishishan County, Gansu*. Kunming: Yunnan University Press.
FENG LIANGFANG (ed.)
2000 *Man People: the Investigation of Shuigouwa village of Baoshang city, Yunnan.* Kunming: Yunnan University Press.
GEERTZ, CLIFFORD
1993 *The Interpretation of Cultures: Selected Essays*. London: Fontana Press. [Translation by Na Ribilige, Shanghai: People Press, 1999.]
GUANGXI CPPCC REVIEW GROUP
2002 'Sufficiently exercise the function of CPPCC of taking part in the discussion and management of state affairs, positively start racial religious work.' *Journal of Guangxi Socialism College* 1: 30-1.

HE SIQIANG, ed.
2000 *Hani People: the Investigation of Luobie village of Luchun County, Yunnan*. Kunming: Yunnan University Press.
HORN, Norbert
2006 *Einführung in die Rechtswissenschaft und Rechtsphilosophie*. Heidelberg: Müller [Translation of 3rd ed. by Luo Li, 2005, Beijing: Legal Press].
HOU JUNSHENG and TAN JIANGHUA
2004 'An Analysis on Authority Transformation in Typical Religious Ethnic Village.' *Social Science* 1: 65-71.
KEESING, Roger M.
1976 *Cultural Anthropology : A Contemporary Perspective*. New York etc: Holt, Rinehart and Winston [Translation by Zhang Gongqi, Taiwan: Juliu Books, 1993].
LI YIYUAN
1997 'Function of Ancestor Worship in Modern Society.' *Human's Perspectives*. Shanghai: Literature Press.
LIANG HONGFEI, trans.
2003 *Society and Religion*. By Chitiandazuo [Japan], B.Walson. Chengdu: Sichuan People Press.
LIU ZHIMING and DENG FEI
2006a 'Xu wenku and His "religion realm".' *Phoenix Weekly* 11: 18-21.
2006b 'Religion Actuality in a village.' *Phoenix Weekly* 11:22-23.
LIANG ZHIPING
2003 'Folk Law in Chinese Legal History-Legal Pluralism in Ancient China.' *Ponder on Fringe*. Beijing: Legal Press.
LU QUN
2006 'Features of Primitive Religions in Ethnic Minorities of China.' *Journal of Jishou University* 1.
LV DAJI and ZHANG SHIHUI
2004 'Religion is a Form of Culture.' *Ethnics of China* 3rd ed. 24 Aug.
LV ZHAOYI and HONG MEI (ed.)
2004 *Menba People: the Investigation of Gongri village of Cuona County, Tibet*. Kunming: Yunnan University Press.
MALINOWSKI, Bronislaw
1922 *Argonauts of the western Pacific: An Account of Native Enterprise and Adventure in the Archipelagoes of Melanesian New Guinea*. London: Routledge & Kegan Paul [Translation by Liang Yongjia and Lee Shaomin, Beijing: Huaxia Press, 2002].

MERRY, Sally Engle
1988 'Legal Pluralism.' *Law and Society Review* 22: 869-96.
MOU ZHONGJIAN
2005 'Ethnic Religion and Social Harmony.' *Chinese Religion* 4:7-10.
NA QI
2001 *Conformity between Tradition and Modern Times: Outline of History, Culture and Development of Hui People in Yunnan*. Kunming: Yunnan University Press.
NIU SHULIN
2005 'Understanding the World by Religion.' *Zhongzhou Journal* 2:135-41.
PEOPLE'S DAILY (CHINA) COMMENTATOR
2004 'To protect civic freedom of religious belief in a lawful way.' *Legal Sound* 1: 10-11.
QUMUYUZHI and LIU YAOHAN (eds.).
1998 *Cases of Customary Law of Yi People in Liangshsan*. Kunming: Yunnan People Press.
RÜTHERS, Bernd
2008 *Rechtstheorie*, 4th ed. München: C.H. Beck. [Translation of 3rd ed. by Ding Xiaochun. Beijing: Legal Press.]
TAN XIAOJIAN (ed.)
2000 *Bulang People: the Investigation of Xinman'e village of Mangang County, Yunnan*. Kunming: Yunnan University Press.
WANG JIAO (ed.)
2000 *Jingpo People: the Investigation of Dengga village of Ruili, Yunnan*. Kunming: Yunnan University Press.
WANG LIANFANG
1998 'Memoir of Mr. Wang Lianfang on Racial Work.' *Racial Unity* 2.
WANG QILIANG
2001 'The Breakdown of Traditional Legal Culture and Absence of Modern Legal Rule: Case Study in a Community .' *Thinking* 5: 87-93.
2004 'What is Law: a Classified System of Arranging Order.' *Modern Legal Science* 4: 98-103.
2006 'Norms system and Realization of Social Order in the Grass-root Village.' *Journal of Nationalities college of Guangxi* 1: 121-26.
WANG QILIANG, LI NA and YU QIANG
2003 'On Problems and Governance of Public Health in Minority Villages: A Fieldwork Report from Yunnan.' In *Collected Papers of a Study of the Law of Regional National Autonomy*. Kunming: Yunnan University Press.

WANG XIAOZHU (ed.)
2000 *Lahu People: the Investigation of laozhai village of Lancing County, Yunnan*. Kunming: Yunnan University Press.
WANG ZHILIANG (ed.)
2000 *Achang People: the Investigation of Mangdong Down village of Dehong, Yunnan*. Kunming: Yunnan University Press.
XIAO YING (ed.)
2000 *Lisu People: the Investigation of Baihualing village of Lushui County, Yunnan*. Kunming: Yunnan University Press.
YANG XUEZHENG
1991 *On Primitive Religions*. Kunming: Yunnan People Press.
YAO JIDE (ed.)
2000 *Hui People: the Investigation of Guzhen village of Tonghai County, Yunnan*. Kunming: Yunnan University Press.
YIN YONGLIN (ed.)
2000 *Miao People: the Investigation of Datanzi village of Jinping County, Yunnan*. Kunming: Yunnan University Press.
ZHANG JIMIN (ed.)
1993 *Collection of Customary Law in Tibet Area of Qinghai*. Qianghai: People Press.
ZHANG XIAOHUI (ed.)
2000 *Dai People: the Investigation of Mangang village of Menhai County, Yunnan*. Kunming: Yunnan University Press.
ZHANG XIAOHUI and WANG QILIANG
2005 'Social Control and Legal Rule in Ethnic Village.' *Thinking* 2: 111-17.
ZHANG YONGHE
2006 *Belief and Authority*. Beijing: Legal Press.
ZHAO MEI (ed.)
2000 *Nu People: the Investigation of Chalashe village of Gongshan County, Yunnan*. Kunming: Yunnan University Press.
ZHENG WEICHUAN (ed.)
2000 *Dulong People: the Investigation of Xiaochala village of Gongshan County, Yunnan*. Kunming: Yunnan University Press.
ZHOU XING (trans.)
1998 *Folk Religion of Han People*. By Dubianxinxiong [Japan]. Tianjin: People Press.
ZHU HESHUANG and XIE ZUO (ed.)
2004 *Sala People: the Investigation of Stone po village of Xunhua County, Qinghai*. Kunming: Yunnan University Press.

MOVING BEYOND THE HIERARCHICAL APPROACH TO LEGAL PLURALISM IN THE SOUTH PACIFIC[1]

Jennifer Corrin

Introduction

In countries of the South Pacific, societies are often discussed in terms of the dichotomy between 'traditional' and 'modern'. Similarly, legal systems are often described by reference to the dichotomy between 'customary' or 'traditional' law and 'state law', and between 'informal' and 'formal' justice. In fact, these divisions are becoming a thing of the past, gradually blurred by changes in the pattern of society and by the interaction between different systems of law. Further, the approach taken to the accommodation of customary law, which has been to formally 'recognise' it in constitutions, has, at least in theory, put an end to its independent operation. In the search for a more effective approach to legal pluralism, the existing dichotomy may often obscure a more complex interplay between the interwoven spheres of 'traditional law' and 'state law' and a new sphere of 'blended' law. In each of these spheres there are uncertainties, including questions of definition and scope, which constitute a potentially destabilising factor and have significant rule of law implications.

Commencing with an overview of the different sources and types of law within the 'customary' and 'state' law spheres in the South Pacific region, this paper

[1] The research assistance of Ms Sarah-Jane Bennett in the preparation of this paper is gratefully acknowledged.

discusses some of the uncertainties and tensions that arise from pluralism in practice. Examples drawn mainly from Solomon Islands are used to illustrate the various ways in which the lines between customary law and state law have been blurred. Outside Papua New Guinea (where there have been significant initiatives to promote custom: see e.g. the Underlying Law Act 2000 (PNG)), Solomon Islands is arguably the South Pacific country that has made the greatest effort to promote customary law, which has resulted in a wide range of examples from which to draw. (See further Corrin Care 2002: 33-34.)

The South Pacific Region: Context and Culture

Pacific Island countries stretch across the Pacific Ocean, from Northern Mariana Islands in the north-west to Pitcairn in the south-east. These countries can be grouped broadly, according to ethnic, cultural and linguistic concepts, into sub-regions of Melanesia, Micronesia and Polynesia. This categorisation is not without controversy, as the diversity of culture, social organisation and practices defies sub-regional boundaries, varying from country to country and, particularly within Melanesia, from island to island, and even from village to village. The number of languages spoken provides some measure of diversity. Papua New Guinea has about 680 languages and Vanuatu 108; in Solomon Islands there are about 65 vernacular languages and dialects in existence.

Social and economic changes have had a profound impact on customary societies. Increased communication with other parts of the world, access to the international media, ease of travel and education are just some factors that have influenced change (Crocombe and Meleisea 1994: Chap. 1). Many people have moved from village to urban life and may no longer feel bound by customary rules. Notwithstanding, there is extensive evidence of the continued existence and strength of the customary law throughout the region, particularly in isolated areas.

The South Pacific Region: Law and Legal Systems

Most of the island countries of the South Pacific are common law jurisdictions.[2]

[2] Non-common law jurisdictions include the Overseas Territories of France, eg, New Caledonia and Easter Island. Vanuatu inherited both common law and civil law. See further Corrin (1998).

Their constitutions are stated to be the supreme law. The power to enact legislation is devolved by the constitution to the national legislature (e.g., Constitution of Solomon Islands 1978, s 58) and national courts are empowered to carry out judicial functions. However, in most cases, foreign statutes in force at the time of independence have been retained in force,[3] together with 'English' common law and equity (Corrin and Paterson 2007: 32-34) and 'colonial' legislation (a term used to refer to law made locally, prior to Independence, by a person or body with legislative power bestowed by England), so far as not excluded by any other law and so far as applicable to the circumstances of the country in question. These laws were intended to fill the void until they were replaced by new laws enacted by the local parliament. Colonial legislation has, in most cases, been patriated, either by the Independence constitution or legislation. The same is not true of foreign statutes which still play a prominent role in the legal systems of many regional countries. In Solomon Islands, for example, the legislature has been slow to act and large areas of law are still governed by English statutes (Corrin Care 2002: 34). This may be compared to Samoa, where only a handful of foreign statutes remain in force (Samoa 1977: Notes to Reprint of Statutes Act 1972), and Tonga where the application of English Statutes was terminated in 2003 (Civil Laws (Amendment) Act 2003). National courts have also been slow to forge their own path, largely being content to follow English common law rather than exploring a local jurisprudence more appropriate to local culture.

As mentioned above, most regional constitutions give recognition to customary law, rendering it a formal source of law.[4] However, it is important to stress that customary law does not rely on constitutional recognition for its validity. It was in force prior to colonisation and co-existed during the colonial period with the acquiescence of authorities. (See e.g. in relation to Solomon Islands and Vanuatu, Brown 2005: 38-40.) Outside of urban centres, however, for many individuals and communities customary law is still *the law*. In this context, the discussion of legal

---

[3] For example, in Fiji Islands the date is 2 January 1875: Supreme Court Ordinance 1876, s 35; in Solomon Islands it is 7 July 1978: Constitution of Solomon Islands 1978, Sch 3, para 4(1); in Vanuatu it is 30 July 1980: Constitution of Vanuatu 1980, Art 95(2). In the case of Vanuatu, French law was also 'saved'.

[4] See for example, Constitution of Solomon Islands 1978, Sch 3, para 3(1); Constitution of Samoa 1960, Art 111(1); Constitution of Vanuatu 1980, Art 47(1). See further Corrin Care 1999.

pluralism from the premise of a hierarchy of laws with state law at the apex, below which other sources are nested (Benton 2002: 8), is misleading. A hierarchical approach assumes the supremacy of the common law and encourages the use of State law as the starting point for the analysis and application of customary law. As Benton points out, such an approach to legal pluralism brings with it "a sense of inevitability about the dominance of state law" (Benton 2002: 9). From the perspective of members of Pacific society in areas where custom is still respected, customary law is paramount. State law is regarded as 'Whiteman's law', which is not their business (Solomon Islands Law Reform Commission 1996: 10-11). Further, as has been pointed out in the anthropological literature, legal systems do not operate in a linear fashion (Ross 1978; Scaglion 1996; White and Lindstrom 1997; see also Stearns 2001). In reality, laws and legal processes are often interwoven and a hierarchical approach obscures the complexities of this relationship. One such complexity arises from the fact that, despite the recognition of customary law and its allocation of a place in the formal hierarchy below statutory law, its precise standing in the state system is often unclear. [5] For example, in a number of South Pacific countries, its relationship with common law and equity is in doubt.[6] In Solomon Islands, for example, whilst it is stated that customary law is to prevail over English common law and equity,[7] in practice it is

[5] See e.g. the following statement of Chief Justice Muria:

> It is a fallacy to view a constitutional principle or a statutory principle as better than those principles contained in customary law. In my view, one is not better than the other. It is the circumstances in which the principles are applied that vary and one cannot be readily substituted for another. (*Pusi v Leni,* unreported, High Court, Solomon Islands, 14 February 1997, available on www.paclii.org at [1997] SBHC 100.)

[6] See e.g. Constitution of Marshall Islands 1978, Art X, ss.1 and 2; Constitution of Samoa 1960, Art III(1); Constitution of Vanuatu, Art 45(1) (discussed Corrin Care 1998: 601-603).

[7] Constitution of Solomon Islands 1978, sch 3, para 2(1)(c):

> [T]he principles and rules of the common law and equity shall have effect as part of the law of Solomon Islands, save in so far as ... in their application to any particular matter, they are inconsistent with customary law applying in respect to the matter.

See also, *Kasa and Kasa v Biku* (unreported, High Court, Solomon Islands, Muria rarely applied by the courts (Corrin and Zorn 2005: 150; Corrin Care and Zorn 2002a: 25, 47, 68). Further, the relationship between customary law and constitutionally enshrined rights is often ambiguous (see further Corrin 2006a, b). Throughout the Pacific, numerous other questions regarding the precise application of customary law remain unresolved (Corrin and Zorn 2005; Corrin Care and Zorn 2002b). These uncertainties have helped to justify those schooled in the common law avoiding the application of customary law despite its formal status. In many cases, it has been bypassed altogether.[8]

Pluralism in the Pacific

The term 'legal pluralism' does not have a single, universally accepted meaning. In the narrow sense it refers to "a situation in which two or more legal systems co-exist in the same social field" of law operating within the same country (Merry 1988: 870; see also Griffiths 1986: 38). In the wider sense it means much more than this. Sack suggests that it involves an ideological commitment in the form of opposition to monism, dualism and any other form of dogmatism or, for those who are opposed to plurality of laws, "a series of essentially undesirable compromises" of a situation that must be "temporarily tolerated as a necessary evil" (Sack 1986: 1).

In countries of the South Pacific, legal pluralism is often discussed by reference to the dichotomy between 'customary' or 'traditional law' and 'state law', and between 'informal' and 'formal' justice. This approach limits legal pluralism to the confines of post-colonial theory and ignores the scholarship on 'new legal pluralism' which acknowledges that the concept is not limited to developing countries (Merry 1988: 872; see further Greenhouse and Strijbosch 1993, which contains articles about legal pluralism in industrialized societies). Further and more pertinently for the present discussion, the 'customary'/'state' law dichotomy misrepresents the South Pacific position. In contrast with many other parts of the common law world, this is not a question of law endorsed by the state as opposed

CJ, 14 January 2000, available at www.paclii.org at [2000] SBHC 62.

[8] See e.g. *Banga v Waiwo* (unreported, Supreme Court, Vanuatu, Vaudin d' Imecourt CJ, 17 June 1996, available at www.paclii.org at [1996] VUSC 5), where Vaudin d'Imecourt C.J. took the view that customary law was a source of last resort, only to be applied in the absence of any other applicable law.

to unofficial law, as most regional constitutions have recognised customary law as an official source of law (e.g. Constitution of Solomon Islands 1978, s. 75, Sch 3, para 3). In this sense, customary law is both state law and part of the formal justice system, operating within the same legal system as the written law.

Moreover, a one dimensional approach to legal pluralism does not acknowledge the other layers of pluralism that operate to deny the legitimacy of the customary law versus state law distinction. Changes in the patterns of society, caused by factors such as greater mobility, access to the media, and the onslaught of Western ideas, have weakened the boundaries between customary law and state law. More pertinently for this paper, the boundaries have been further eroded by interaction between the different types of law. This 'blurring' process occurs in a number of ways. Perhaps the most obvious of these, and the focus of this paper, is where legislators attempt to incorporate or accommodate customary law in statute law. Another is where the state courts purport to apply common law or statute in a way that interstitially takes account of customary law.[9] Less obviously, the reverse may occur: courts may purport to apply customary law, but do so in such a way that they are treating it as common law (Corrin 2008).

Legislative efforts to incorporate customary law often occur on an ad hoc basis rather than as part of a well thought-out scheme. They are frequently the result of individual effort rather than a comprehensive government policy. This often results in a failure to take account of the differences between the culture and processes surrounding the customary and formal legal systems, and the lack of provision of mechanisms for overcoming the conflicts that inevitably arise. Thus for example, a requirement to take account of customary law leaves the court to struggle with the question of what exactly that law entails and how it is to be pleaded and proved (see further Corrin Care and Zorn 2002a). These omissions partly explain the third manifestation of the blending process, that is, the tendency to equate customary law with the nearest common law equivalent.

The following sections of this article seek to illustrate the multi-layered pluralism at work within the South Pacific by giving practical examples of the first of the three manifestations of the blurring process, that is, legislative attempts to incorporate or accommodate customary law in statute law. The examples chosen illustrate not only the process, but also the failure to take account of underlying

[9] For an interesting example from Micronesia see *Pohnpei v Weilbacher* (5 FSM Intrm 431 (Pon S Ct Tr 1992)).

differences and the practical conundrums posed by legal pluralism in the South Pacific.

Attempts to Incorporate Customary Law in Statutes

In several instances legislators have sought to incorporate customary law in statute. The most comprehensive example of this is in Fiji, where customary law on the holding and use of land, fishing rights and chiefly titles has been embodied in statute. The 1997 Constitution lists these statutes and entrenches them,[10] providing that a Bill to amend these Acts must be read three times in each House and be supported by at least nine of the fourteen members of Senate appointed by the *Bose Levu Vakaturaga* (The Great Council of Chiefs). Attempting to codify custom or encapsulate wide areas of customary law in statutes has its own problems which have been discussed elsewhere (e.g. Corrin Care and Zorn 2002a: 10, 47-48). This section looks at less ambitious initiatives.

A number of problems arise from attempts to incorporate customary law in statute. Apart from the question as to whether customary law is still customary once it is in statutory form (Corrin Care and Zorn 2002a: 10, 47-48), merely providing for the application of customary law without any guidance on how this is to be achieved arguably leaves the courts with a square peg to fit into a round hole. This issue and other difficulties that have arisen are illustrated by the following two particularly graphic examples, both from Solomon Islands. The first looks at legislation designed to deal with determination of customary land rights, and the second at an attempt to integrate customary law on succession into the National Provident Scheme.

Local Courts Act and the Forest Resources and Timber Utilisation Act

In many countries of the region 'customary courts' have been established by

---

[10] The Constitution of the Republic of the Fiji Islands 1997, enacted by the Constitution Amendment Act 1997, 185(1). The Acts are the Fijian Affairs Act, Cap 120; Fijian Development Fund Act, Cap 121; Native Lands Act, Cap 133; Native Land Trust Act, Cap 134; Rotuma Act, Cap 122 ; Rotuman Lands Act, Cap 138; Banaban Lands Act, Cap 124; and Banaban Settlement Act, Cap 123.

legislation. The aim of establishing such courts is to provide a more flexible and informal forum for resolution of disputes. These courts are only 'customary' in the sense that they administer customary law. They are not traditional forums and in reality they are often adversarial, or at least overly formal, and do not resolve issues in a customary way.[11]

One such 'customary court' is the Local Court in Solomon Islands, A Local Court has jurisdiction to deal with minor disputes arising within the geographical area for which it is constituted and exclusive jurisdiction to deal with all proceedings of a civil nature affecting or arising in connection with customary land.[12] In 1985, the limitations of 'customary' courts were recognised and the Local Courts Act was amended by the Local Courts (Amendment) Act 1985. This landmark piece of legislation sought to have ownership of customary land decided in a customary way, rather than in a 'customary' court established on a Western model. This statutory amendment to the process for determining customary land disputes provides a good example of an attempt to incorporate customary processes into the formal court process. It also provides an example of how well-intentioned reforms do not always produce desirable results.

The amending Act attempted to return some of the decision-making on customary land matters to traditional leaders by making referral to the chiefs a prerequisite for lodging a claim with the Local Courts. Thus, Local Courts only have power to hear customary land disputes where:

> the dispute has first been referred to the chiefs;
> all traditional means of resolving the dispute have been exhausted; and
> the chiefs have made no decision wholly acceptable to both parties (Local Courts Act Cap 19, s 12).

[11] For example, Vanuatu's Island Courts are subject to the following procedural rules: Island Courts (Civil Procedure) Rules 2005, Island Courts (Court Clerks) Rules 2005, Island Courts (Criminal Procedure) Rules 2005, Island Courts (Supervising Magistrates) Rules 2005.

[12] Land and Titles Act, Cap 133 s 254. There are exceptions to this jurisdiction: matters expressly excluded by the Land and Titles Act and questions as to whether land is or not customary land.

However, there are difficulties with the procedure, not least the unwillingness of unsuccessful parties to abide by the chiefs' decision. This has led to an increase in litigation rather than a reduction. There have also been difficulties in ascertaining the identity of the 'chiefs' in some areas of the country.[13]

A further problem was exposed by the recent case of *Majoria v Jino*.[14] In this case it was pointed out that, whilst it was clear that referral to the chiefs was a prerequisite to lodging a claim with the Local Court, the status of any decision made by the chiefs had not been specified. In order to explain the facts of this case it is necessary to say something about the legislative scheme for the acquisition of timber rights in Solomon Islands, which is provided by the Forest Resources and Timber Utilisation Act (Cap. 40) of Solomon Islands.

The Forest Resources and Timber Utilisation Act is a further example of a statute that seeks to accommodate customary law, but a less benevolent measure than the other legislation discussed in this section. The statute was enacted to by-pass the problems that had arisen in getting permission to log customary land. It provides a process for identifying those entitled to grant 'timber rights' in respect of customary land. Under the original scheme the initial determination was made by the area council (Forest Resources and Timber Utilisation Act, s. 8, prior to its amendment by the Forest Resources and Timber Utilisation (Amendment) Act 2000). That power is now exercised by the Provincial Executive, and appeals against decisions can be made to the Customary Land Appeal Court (Forest Resources and Timber Utilisation Act, s 10(1)). Following the enactment of the Forest Resources and Timber Utilisation Act there are now two separate bodies dealing with customary land tenure: one determining customary land 'ownership', and the other the right to grant timber rights. This distinction recognises that customary land tenure is multi-layered (Corrin 2008). The relationship between timber rights 'owners' and customary 'landowners' is not specified in either Act. However, it has been the subject of a number of court decisions. The position, as it was understood to be until the case of *Majoria v Jino,* was well explained thus

[13] See e.g., *Nelson Lauringi and Others v Lagwaeano Sawmilling and Logging Limited and Others* (unreported, High Court, Solomon Islands, Lungole-Awich J, 28 August 1997, available at www.paclii.org at [1997] SBHC 61).

[14] Unreported, Court of Appeal, Solomon Islands, Lord Slynn of Hadley P., Adams J.A., Salmon J.A., 1 November 2007, available at www.paclii.org at [2007] SBCA 20).

by Ward C.J:

> the Forest Resources and Timber Utilisation Act as amended, sets up a procedure whereby anybody wishing to acquire timber rights over customary land can identify the people with whom to deal. The procedure identifies persons to represent the group as a whole. Once the procedure has been followed, the people named by the area council are the only people entitled to sign an agreement to transfer those rights and that are clearly, as the parties to the agreement, the people to whom the royalties should be paid. ... I have no way of knowing, on the evidence before me, whether the persons identified by the Area Council as entitled to grant timber rights have that entitlement because they are landowners or because they have some secondary rights and neither can I question their decision on that. (*Tovua v Meki* [1988/89] SILR 74: 76.)

In *Majoria v Jino* the court was required to consider the relationship between the Local Courts Act and the Forest Resources and Timber Utilisation Act in respect of determination of customary land rights. The facts of the case were that, in 2002, the appellant and other named members of the Kadiki tribe were determined by the Western Provincial Executive to be the holders of timber rights in a specified area referred to as 'Rodo Customary Land'. The respondent and other members of the Bareke tribe lodged an appeal against this decision to the Customary Land Appeal Court (Western) (WCLAC). In 2003, prior to any determination by the WCLAC, the matter was referred to the Marovo Council of Chiefs, who determined that only the Kadiki tribe had any rights over 'Rodo Customary Land'. In May 2005, the appellant commenced High Court proceedings against the respondent, representing the Bareke Tribe, and the WCLAC, challenging the jurisdiction of the WCLAC to hear the appeal against the Western Provincial Executive's decision. In the same month, the Western Provincial Executive approved a timber rights agreement between the Appellant and other members of the Kadiki tribe and Rodo Development Company (RDC), and RDC was granted a timber licence. The following month, however, the WCLAC quashed the determination made by the Western Provincial Executive, holding that it failed to comply with the Forest Resources and Timber Utilisation Act, which required it to determine the holders of the timber rights, and the nature and extent of the rights to be granted (Forest Resources and Timber Utilisation Act, s 8. The Western Provincial Executive's determination in 2002 would appear to have satisfied the requirement of s 8). The WCLAC, however, made no determination of ownership of the land in question.

In the High Court proceedings, heard in 2007, the respondent, sought to establish that a parcel of land known as 'Havahava Customary Land', lying within the boundaries of Rodo Customary land, belonged to the Bareke tribe rather than the Kadiki tribe. Brown J held that the decision of the Marovo Council of Chiefs that Havahava land was part of Rodo land, was made under a different regime (i.e. the Land and Titles Act and the Local Courts Act) and was not binding on the WCLAC, which was acting under the regime created by the Forest Resources and Timber Utilisation Act.

The appellants appealed to the Court of Appeal, challenging the decision and seeking determination of the significance of the 2003 decision of the Marovo Council of Chiefs. The Court of Appeal stated that where a decision is made by the WCLAC as to customary ownership of land as a necessary preliminary to determining the disposal of timber rights, that decision is binding on the parties. However, in this case the decision of the Marovo Council of Chiefs was given before the WCLAC made its decision. Therefore, the status of the decision of the Marovo Council of Chiefs was a crucial issue. The Court of Appeal noted that the statutory scheme was not 'entirely easy to interpret' and considered it particularly unfortunate that the status of a decision of the Chiefs was not explicitly stated in the legislation. However, the court considered that

> ... the key to understanding the scheme and applying it in a practical way is to recognise the important role assigned by the Parliament to the Chiefs and their decisions for the purpose of determining disputes of customary land.

They went on to say:

> If the party who succeeded before the Chiefs is left in the situation that the other party can simply act as though that decision had never occurred, that would tend to discourage attempts to settle disputes by traditional means. It would encourage parties with weak cases to ignore a summons by the Chiefs to hearings or not to take the Chiefs seriously, in the knowledge that any adverse decision will not affect them. It would tend seriously to undermine the authority of the Chiefs, a

> result that is obviously the very opposite of that intended by the legislative scheme. It would also encourage multiplication of litigation. It follows, as we think, that a party who disagrees with a decision of the Chiefs but who declines to take advantage of the legislative scheme for reconsidering that determination by invoking the jurisdiction of the local court must be considered to be bound by the decision. (*Majoria v Jino*[15])

As can be seen from this decision, the legislative regimes introduced by the Local Courts Act and the Forest Resources and Timber Utilisation Act to deal with interests in customary land are far from clear. The position is exacerbated when the two schemes come into contact, as each Act has been devised in isolation from the other and little thought appears to have been given to their interaction. The Court of Appeal, left to deal with the resulting conflict appears to have been well motivated, acknowledging that resolution of disputes over customary land was 'of vital importance to the people, their communities and the country' and that therefore, it was the duty of the courts to make the legislative scheme work if this could be done consistently with the language of the statutes. Further, the Court appears to have been willing to accommodate the demands of legal pluralism, stating that, 'the key to understanding the scheme and applying it in a practical way is to recognise the important role assigned by the Parliament to the Chiefs and their decisions for the purpose of determining disputes of customary land'. However, as in many other instances the Court appears to be dominated by a hierarchical approach, taking the common law on land tenure as a starting point. In particular, it has assumed that the rights being determined under the Local Courts Act are the same as those being determined under the Forest Resources and Timber Utilisation Act. According to earlier case law, they clearly are not (*Allardyce Lumber Company Ltd v Attorney General*[16]). If the courts cannot grasp the subtleties involved in customary land tenure and legislators cannot adequately accommodate the relevant law in the formal system, a significant barrier is posed for customary 'landowners' wanting to enforce their rights.

It is also relevant to note that the litigation between the parties to *Majoria v Jino,*

---

[15] Above note 14.

[16] Unreported, High Court, Solomon Islands, Ward CJ,18 August 1989, available at www.paclii.org at [1989] SBHC 1.

over the same area of customary land, is continuing in the High Court[17] and the Court of Appeal[18]. Although the dispute is primarily about customary land, which the Land and Titles Act clearly states is to be governed by customary law,[19] the dispute resolution process is dominated by the common law forms of relief, procedure and forum. Customary law and dispute resolution processes are again marginalised in favour of the dominant common law system and the legislation fails dismally in its aim of accommodation.

It should also be noted that there are reforms on foot in this area. The Tribal Land Dispute Resolution Bill 2008, an ambitious foray into statutory accommodation of customary processes in the formal system of land dispute resolution, is currently out for consultation in Solomon Islands. The Bill is intended to provide a new forum for determination of customary land disputes, but in its current form it is badly drafted and gives rise to its own set of problems, which are outside the scope of this paper.

Solomon Islands National Provident Fund Act

Another prominent example of a statutory amendment designed to take into account customary laws is the Solomon Islands National Provident Fund Act (Cap. 109). This Act provides for the establishment of a national provident fund ('SINPF'), which operates as a compulsory self-funded pension scheme. Funds are derived from compulsory contributions to the fund by employers and employees, which are invested and paid out to the employee on turning fifty or on retirement. It also provides that members of the fund may nominate a person to whom they

[17] *Majoria v Jino,* unreported, High Court, Solomon Islands, Faukona J., 16 May 2008, available at www.paclii.org at [2008] SBHC 54.

[18] *Majoria v Jino,* unreported, Court of Appeal, Solomon Islands, Goldsborough P., Williams J.A., Hansen J.A., 26 March 2009, available at www.paclii.org at [2009] SBCA 4.

[19] Land and Titles Act Cap 133, s. 239(1):

> The manner of holding, occupying, using, enjoying and disposing of customary land shall be in accordance with the current customary usage applicable thereto, and all questions relating thereto shall be determined accordingly.

wish their entitlement to be paid in the event of the member's death. However, a nomination is invalidated by a subsequent marriage (Solomon Islands National Provident Fund Act Cap 109, s. 32). Originally, it was provided that, in the absence of a valid nomination, distribution would be in accordance with the intestacy provisions in the Wills, Probate and Administration Act (Cap. 33). Those provisions take no account of customary obligations, and only provide for distribution in accordance with 'Western' nuclear family values and relationships. In 1990, the national parliament amended the Act to make it more appropriate to the circumstances of Solomon Islands (Solomon Islands National Provident Fund (Amendment) Act 1990, s. 6). The amendment provides that, where a member of SINPF dies without a valid nomination in place, distribution is to be "in accordance with the custom of the member to the children, spouse and other persons entitled thereto in accordance with that custom" (Solomon Islands National Provident Fund (Amendment) Act 1990, s. 33(c)).

This effort to accommodate customary law within the formal system is no doubt an appropriate measure in a country where customary law has more resonance than state law. However, the introduction of this type of provision without any direction as to process has led to difficulties. This is well illustrated by the case of *Tanavulu and Tanavulu v Tanavulu and SINPF.*[20] In that case, the deceased had nominated his brother and nephew as beneficiaries when he joined the fund. When he married the following year, that nomination became void. After he died, the deceased's father applied for and was paid the amount held in the fund ($11,079) on the basis of custom in Babatana, South Choiseul. The father deposited $4,000 in an interest-bearing deposit account in the name of the deceased's son. He paid $2,000 each to the deceased's brother and nephew. He used $3,000 to meet funeral expenses and $79 for his own purposes. The deceased's widow, who had received nothing, challenged this distribution in the High Court, seeking a declaration that she and her infant child were entitled to one third of the money each. She also alleged that

[20] Unreported, High Court, Solomon Islands, Lungole-Awich J, 12 January 1998), available at www.paclii.org at [1998] SBHC 4. For other discussions of this case see: Corrin 2006a; Brown and Corrin Care 2001: 668-670; Corrin Care and Zorn 2005: 155-158. See also the Solomon Islands case *The Minister for Provincial Government v Guadalcanal Provincial Assembly*, unreported, High Court, Solomon Islands, Kapi P., Williams J.A., Goldsbrough J.A., 11 July 1997, available at www.paclii.org at [1997] SBCA 1, where the Court of Appeal refused to declare an Act which discriminated against women unconstitutional. This decision is discussed in detail in Brown and Corrin Care 2001.

SINPF had been negligent in carrying out their duties under the Act.

The case raised several questions in relation to customary law. First, who was entitled in custom; second which custom was to be applied and how was the existence of such law to be proved; and third, what was the position where such law conflicted with fundamental rights. With regard to the first question, SINPF did not make any inquiries as to the prevailing customary law, but merely required a form to be completed with personal particulars, including the applicant's relationship to the deceased, and witnessed by a person who knew the applicant personally, together with a statutory declaration stating the applicant's relationship to the deceased and the basis for his claim in custom. Awich J considered that, having received this information, SINPF had complied with its duty and stated: "It would be absurd to expect NPF to hold elaborate inquiries that may involve travelling to the village of every deceased member or gathering witnesses in order to determine what a particular custom is." Whilst there is some truth in this, acting on a signed form and statutory declaration from an interested party, hardly qualifies as an inquiry at all.

At trial, the widow's challenged the father's version of the applicable custom. Customary law differs from place to place within Solomon Islands. In this case the custom was that of the deceased's home village of Babatana. It was not disputed that inheritance in that area was patrilineal, but the witnesses differed as to whether the deceased's father had a complete discretion to distribute the estate or whether the money should be paid to the deceased's son, with an unspecified share to be paid as of right to the mother. There was no guidance in the Act as to how customary law should be proved. The judge appears to have assumed that, in the event of dispute, proof of custom was a matter for oral evidence. The widow gave evidence herself and called one other witness on custom. The deceased's father gave evidence of custom and called two witnesses to support him, one male and one female. The judgment gives no details of how these witnesses were qualified to give evidence or what factors the court considered relevant to such competence. The court preferred the evidence of the deceased's father and his witnesses, according to which the deceased's father was entitled to distribute the proceeds of the fund to relatives as he saw fit. It was held that the children and spouse had no automatic right to payment, as they would have done if the fund had formed part of the deceased's estate on intestacy. The deceased's father had the discretion to pay some amount of the inheritance to the widow but this was not obligatory. In some circumstances, such as where the widow left the father's house, as she had done here, he was entitled to leave her out of the distribution altogether.[21]

The third issue is perhaps an even more serious tension arising from pluralism that will often form a hurdle to accommodation of customary law in the state system. Given that customary law is underpinned by patriarchal and status based norms how can this be reconciled with a constitutional commitment to human rights? In this case it was argued on behalf of the widow that the rules of customary law should not govern the distribution of funds as they were discriminatory. Section 15 of the Solomon Islands Constitution provides protection from discrimination, and 'law' which offends against it is unconstitutional. However, the judge found that the word 'law' in section 15(1), did not include customary law. His basis for this finding was that the words, 'no law shall', in section 15(1), were referring to a law to be made in the future. As customary law was 'evolving or was already pertaining [by which it is assumed His Lordship meant 'existing'] at the time of the adoption of the Constitution' it was not such a law. According to this decision, no customary law, no matter how discriminatory, would be outlawed by section 15. Awich J went on to say that even if sub-section (1) had included customary law, section 15(5)(c) and section 15(5)(d) would excuse discriminatory law in a case such as this. Section 15(5)(c) exempts certain personal law, including law 'with respect to devolution of property on death', from the protection against discrimination. The reasoning in this case is open to serious question, as discussed elsewhere (Corrin2006a).

On appeal, the Court of Appeal agreed with the trial judge's conclusions: whether or not the spouse and child received a share was 'dependent upon custom'. On the conflict between customary law and protection from discrimination, the Court of Appeal limited itself to upholding the trial judge's decision on the basis that section 15(5) recognised that the application of customary law might have certain

[21] In some areas the wife is expected to remain with the husband's family after his death, if there are children of the marriage. If she leaves, the bride price may have to be returned and she runs the risk of losing all rights (see further *To'ofilu v Oimae,* unreported, High Court, Solomon Islands, Palmer J, 19 June 1997, available at www.paclii.org at [1997] SBHC 33). The attitude that the wife is expected to live with the husband's family during his lifetime has prevailed outside the customary sphere in Fiji Islands, where a wife was refused a divorce on the grounds of constructive desertion and cruelty when she left the matrimonial home as she could not put up with her mother in law's presence: *Begum v Hussein,* unreported, Magistrates' Court, Fiji Islands (Suva), Civil Case 198/1989.

discriminatory consequences.

In addition to the three issues aired in the case, there are two other unanswered questions posed by the legislation. First, does customary law cease to apply if parties no longer feel bound by customary law? Many islanders who move from their home village for education, work or marriage become divorced from the customary system. In *Tanavulu v Tanavulu*[22] this may well have been the case. It is revealed that both the deceased and the appellant were both educated and lived and worked in Honiara, the deceased in human resources for a government ministry and the appellant as a nurse. They were married in Honiara in a Methodist church. The second, related question is what is the position in the case of an expatriate or some other person who does not belong to a customary community. The Act makes no provision to deal with this situation, although there are many non-islanders contributing to the fund. Common sense would suggest their entitlement should be distributed in accordance with their will or under the intestacy rules if they fail to make a valid nomination, but until this question is considered by the courts the position is uncertain.

Therefore, whilst the Solomon Islands National Provident Fund Act seeks to acknowledge the importance of customary law for members of Solomon Islands society, it does so without adequate provision for resolving the issues that it raises.

Conclusion

It is clear from the legislation and case law discussed above that a one dimensional, hierarchical approach to legal pluralism prevails in the South Pacific. The existing dichotomy between 'customary' and 'state law' is an unhelpful way to proceed and has hampered reform. Although much has been said and written about the promotion of customary law and South Pacific jurisprudence, in practice little progress has been made since independence. The problems created then, when diverse systems of law were forced to live together, without any guidance on the manner of their relationship, are no nearer being solved. To date there has been no integrated approach to these dilemmas. Rather the reform process meanders slowly along, driven by ad hoc initiatives, seemingly driven by individual zeal and the

[22] Unreported, High Court, Solomon Islands, Lungole-Awich J, 12 January 1998, available at www.paclii.org at [1998] SBHC 4.

'outputs' focus of donors. In each of these spheres there are uncertainties, including questions of definition and scope, which constitute a potentially destabilising factor and have significant rule of law implications.

The scholarship of legal pluralism has been largely ignored in the South Pacific, even though the emphasis on governance by many aid programmes lends itself to this focus. The approach to law reform requires a paradigm shift. The continued emphasis on the state and the common law and the limitation of legal pluralism to the confines of post-colonial theory fails to obey the constitutional mandate to recognise and promote customary law. Such a dramatic change is also hampered by the lack of an appropriate philosophical basis from which to proceed and effort needs to be concentrated on discovering exactly what South Pacific jurisprudence entails. As stated by Narakobi twenty-three years ago,

> If law springs from the cultural fabric of a people, then for it to be effective it must be supported by corresponding moral and social ethics. Universal ethical postulates tend to negate the cultural roots from which Melanesia must emerge. The task of developing a Melanesian jurisprudence thus requires that careful thought is given to identifying and articulating the total cosmic view which is reflected in the Melanesian way of life. (Narakobi 1986: 227)

In the context of customary land reform, the late Ron Crocombe warned against grand schemes for reform in the Pacific (Crocombe 2002) and that is good advice. However, the lack of an appropriate philosophical basis is exactly why such schemes have been doomed to failure in the past. Recognition of the complex legal pluralism at play within the region is a small step towards development of an appropriate philosophy.

References

BENTON, Lauren
2002 *Law and Colonial Cultures: Legal Regimes in World History, 1400-1900.* Cambridge: Cambridge University Press.
BROWN, Kenneth
2005 *Reconciling Customary Law and Received Law in Melanesia.* Darwin:

Charles Darwin University Press.

BROWN, Kenneth and Jennifer CORRIN CARE

2001 'More on Democratic Fundamentals in Solomon Islands: Minister for Provincial Government v Guadalcanal Provincial Assembly.' *Victoria University of Wellington Law Review* 32: 653-671.

CORRIN, Jennifer

1998 'Bedrock and Steel Blues: Finding the Law Applicable in Vanuatu' 24 *Commonwealth Law Bulletin* 24: 594-612.

1999 'Conflict between Customary Law and Human Rights in the South Pacific.' *Commonwealth Law Conference Papers* 1: 251-272.

2002 '"Wisdom and Worthy Customs": Customary Law in the South Pacific' *Reform* 80: 31-36.

2006a 'Negotiating the Constitutional Conundrum: Balancing Cultural Identity with Principles of Gender Equality in Post-Colonial South Pacific Societies' 5 *Indigenous Law Journal* 51-81.

2006b 'A Green Stick or a Fresh Stick? Locating Customary Penalties in the Post-Colonial Era' *Oxford University Commonwealth Law Journal* 6: 27-60.

2008 'Customary Law and the Language of the Common Law.' *Common Law World Review* 37: 305-333.

CORRIN CARE, Jennifer and Jean G. ZORN

2002a *Proving Customary Law in the Common Law Courts of the South Pacific.* London: British Institute of International and Comparative Law.

2002b '"Barava Tru" – Judicial approaches to the pleading and proof of custom in the South Pacific.' *International and Comparative Law Quarterly* 51: 611-639.

2005 'Legislating for the application of customary law in Solomon Islands' *Common Law World Review* 34: 144-168.

CORRIN, Jennifer and Don PATERSON

2007 *Introduction to South Pacific Law*, 2nd ed. Abingdon, England: Routledge-Cavendish.

CROCOMBE, Ron

2002 'Customary Land: Some Lessons for the Future from Past and Present Experiences in the Pacific Region.' Paper presented at the Papua New Guinea Institute of Valuers and Land Administrators Conference, Lae.

CROCOMBE, Ron and Malama MELEISEA (eds.)

1994 *Land Issues in the Pacific.* Suva: Institute for Pacific Studies, University of the South Pacific.

GREENHOUSE, Carol J. and Fons STRIJBOSCH (eds.)
1993 *Special Issue: Legal Pluralism in Industrialized Societies. Journal of Legal Pluralism and Unofficial Law:* 33.
GRIFFITHS, John
1986 'What is Legal Pluralism?' *Journal of Legal Pluralism* 24: 1-55.
MERRY, Sally Engle
1988 'Legal Pluralism.' *Law & Society Review* 22: 869-896.
NARAKOBI, Bernard
1986 'In search of a Melanesian jurisprudence.' Pp. 215-228 in Peter Sack and Elizabeth Minchin (eds), *Legal Pluralism.* Canberra: Australian National University.
SAMOA
1977 Revised Statutes of Samoa.
SOLOMON ISLANDS LAW REFORM COMMISSION
1996 *Annual Report*. Honiara: Solomon Islands Law Reform Commission.
ROSS, H.M.
1978 'Leadership Styles and Strategies in a Traditional Melanesian Society', p. 11 in D.L. Oliver (ed.), *Rank and Status in Polynesia and Melanesia: Essays in Honour of Douglas Oliver.* Paris: Musée de l'homme.
SACK, Peter
1986 'Legal Pluralism: Introductory Comments.' Pp. 1-16 in Peter Sack and Elizabeth Minchin (eds), *Legal Pluralism.* Canberra: Australian National University.
SCAGLION, Richard
1996 'Chiefly Models in Papua New Guinea.' *The Contemporary Pacific* 8: 1-31.
WHITE, Geoffrey M. and Lamont LINDSTROM (eds.)
1997 *Chiefs Today: Traditional Pacific leadership and the post-colonial state.* Stanford CA: Stanford University Press.
STEARNS, Peter N. (gen. ed.)
2001 *Encyclopedia of World History,* 6th ed. New York: Houghton Mifflin Co.

‘GOD IS AN ABSENTEE, TOO’: THE TREATMENT OF *WAQF* (ISLAMIC TRUST) LAND IN ISRAEL/PALESTINE

Haitam Suleiman and Robert Home

Introduction: Legal Pluralism in Israel/Palestine

Greater recognition of *shari'a* law is being called for among jurisdictions with significant Muslim minorities and conditions of legal pluralism. In Europe this may be limited to areas such as family and inheritance law, while in sub-Saharan Africa a wider application is campaigned for. Recent academic work in postcolonial legal geography has also been re-appraising how differentiated territorial jurisdictions marginalize unwanted social groups (Blomley & others 2001). Indigenous groups dispossessed from their communal and ancestral lands are increasingly re-asserting their claims through legal and human rights challenges. This article explores the treatment of Islamic *waqf* property (held for religious charitable purposes) in the Arab/Israeli conflict over land in Israel/Palestine, setting it within a context of postcolonial legal pluralism.

Within the territories that comprise Israel/Palestine[1], land is the central contested issue. The Zionists in the early 20th century regarded Palestine as ‘a land without people for a people without land’, and claimed for themselves a historic and God-

[1] This article refers to Israel/Palestine as the pre-1948 territory of Palestine, which now comprises: the state of Israel; the occupied territories (post-1967) of the West bank, formerly under Jordanian jurisdiction, and the Gaza Strip, formerly under Egyptian jurisdiction; and Jerusalem, with a special and complex legal status.

given mission to 'redeem the land from desolation'. Recent revisionist academic lawyers and historians have relocated the Israeli national story within a colonial and postcolonial narrative (eg Morris 2000, Benvenisti 2002). Israel/Palestine inherits several legal traditions, offering often conflicting sources of legitimacy: Islamic, as applied by the Ottoman empire until 1918, and more recently by Jordan in the West Bank and Egypt in Gaza; British colonial, under the League of Nations Mandate (1923-48); and post-1948 Israeli, with borrowings from United States and European jurisdictions. As stated by Shamir:

> 'Too little attention has also been given to the basic fact that the British, aided by all their colonial experience elsewhere, created and installed a functioning state in Palestine: a rather advanced web of administrative apparatuses and governmental departments, a sound infrastructure and, of course, a fully-developed, ready-to-use legal system' (Shamir 2000: 11).

Israel/Palestine's sacred status to three major religions (Islam, Judaeism and Christianity) also makes the territory uniquely saturated with religious and symbolic significance. The stewardship of land by the different faiths has been a contested area. This article examines the large-scale transfer of *waqf* land, supposedly held in perpetuity, to Jewish control through various legal mechanisms since the creation of the state of Israel in 1948, and recent legal disputes over the status of certain mosques and cemeteries.

The English-language literature on *waqf* in Israel/Palestine is limited, while relevant legislation and court rulings are often unpublished, or unavailable in English. This article is the outcome of field research undertaken by a Palestinian Arab living in Israel (Haitam Suleiman). He had the advantage of full Hebrew, Arabic and English language competence, and familiarity with the local cultural background, all important where questions dealt with controversial and sensitive issues, and when the field-work was sometimes disrupted by the current instabilities.

The *Waqf*: A Stagnant or Reviving Institution?

The Islamic legal system presents an eternally valid ideal towards which society aspires, and thus differs from the Western legal tradition, which separates or reduces the role of religion. *Waqf* [pl. *awqaf*] in Arabic means confinement or prohibition, and in Islamic *shari'a* law is a juridical institution facilitating the reservation of property for religious purposes. A *waqf* is established by a living man or woman (the *waqif* = founder) who holds a certain revenue-producing property, and makes the property inalienable in perpetuity, prohibited from sale, gift and inheritance. The property is placed under the stewardship of a fiduciary (*wali* or *mutawalli*) who assures that the revenues pass to the intended beneficiaries (*mustahiqeen*) (Zarqa 1994; Sait & Lim 2006). Under *shari'a* law, while *sadaqa* (charity) should reach only the poor and needy, *waqf* can be directed to both poor and rich; *Sadaqa* may be owned, sold, or granted, but the *waqf* is perpetual, with no intervention in ownership, and is confined to fixed property, or things that have sustainable reserved revenues.

There are three basic kinds of *waqf*. The first, the *khairy* or charitable *waqf*, directs property revenues towards philanthropic goals. The second, the *ahli* or family *waqf*, benefits family members, with the endower choosing what individuals and what lines of descent benefit; administrators are family members, and the revenue-bearing assets circulate indefinitely. Finally, the *mushtarak* or joint *waqf*, divide the revenues between philanthropy and family.

Ironically, given the contested state of *waqf* in Israel, the very first *waqf* was created by a Jewish convert to Islam who bequeathed his wealth to the Prophet for the benefit of the poor and needy (Akgundfiz 1996: 59). The juridical form of the *waqf* took shape in succeeding centuries, and the jurist Abu Yusuf (d. 798) asserted that a *waqf* was valid only if irrevocable and made in perpetuity (Hennigan 1999). Its perpetuity element distinguishes the *waqf* from the trusts and foundations found in Western legal systems, but it apparently influenced the early English trusts during the time of the crusades, when there was much population movement between Europe and the Holy Lands, including the Franciscan Friars. The University of Oxford in its early years may have been influenced by the *waqf*, with the 1264 Statutes of Merton College (significant in the founding of the college system) showing Islamic influences (Gaudiosi 1988).

Awqaf proliferated with the establishment of Muslim-ruled states, offering a means of diverting resources from consumption, and investing them in productive assets to provide either usufruct or revenues for future consumption by individuals or groups of individuals (Yediyildiz 1990: 35-39; Kahf 1998). *Awqaf* served many functions. They provided educational institutions with buildings, teaching materials, staff salaries, and scholarships for poor students, derived from the revenues of orchards and rental buildings, and independent of the state (Sayed 1989: 249-258). They provided health services, public kitchens, orphanages, environmental protection and animal care (Al Qaradawi 1976). *Awqaf* stimulated economic activity, providing shops at low rent, public water fountains, and accommodation for commercial caravans (Kuran 2004). A range of public goods now provided by government agencies in the past came through private *waqf,* which have been called 'the single most important and pervasive economic institution of Islamic society with profound effects on the tax structure of the state, the redistribution of wealth in society and the urban fabric of Islamic cities' (Peters 1986: 173). The *waqf* was an urban institution that shaped the civic space of Ottoman cities (Van Leeuwen 1999: 203), while *waqf* property was estimated at over a third of the agricultural land in Turkey, Morocco, Egypt and Syria (Kahf 1998).

By the second half of the 19th century the *waqf*'s rigidities made it increasingly inadequate for the provision of public goods, and modernizing states in the Middle East nationalized vast *waqf* properties, while new municipal government services increasingly supplanted the *waqf* (Kahf 1998). Legislation brought *waqf* under greater regulation or absolute prohibition, and contributed to the prevalence of secular law over *shari'a* principles, resulting in the stagnation of *waqf*. The family *waqf* was restricted, and some states forbade new creations, with the stipulations of *waqf* founders no longer treated as 'sacred and inviolable'. The state claimed that the *waqf* was no longer serving its original purposes, and it could administer them better (Sait & Lim 2006: 76). The eclipse of *waqf* has left a vacuum in the arena of public services: students, the sick, homeless, travellers, the poor and prisoners are only some of the vulnerable who have lost the protection of the *waqf*.

The *waqf* is, however, showing signs of reinvigoration, with *awqaf* properties occupying a growing share of the societal wealth of Muslim countries and those with significant Muslim minorities. Since the oil crisis of the 1970s Islamic banking has developed new tools of finance, and *waqf* has emerged as a non-profit 'third' sector, distinct from the profit-based private sector and the official public sector. Its institutional protection is making it again a main actor in the social and economic life of Muslims (Kahf 1998).

'God is an absentee too': The Loss of *Waqf* Land to the State of Israel

Most *waqf* property in Israel has been expropriated by the Israeli state under

Absentee Property Laws, and it is one of the most sensitive and complicated issues in the Palestinian-Israeli conflict. As the Palestinian refugees put it, 'God is an absentee too'. Israel claims 93 per cent of its territory as public domain for the Jewish faith, and the process of confiscation has isolated and contained the surviving Arab communities within Israel, while the rest of the Palestinian people have been displaced to peripheral locations (Gaza, the West Bank), under Israeli military occupation since 1967 (Home 2003).

During the period 1918-48 land dominated the efforts of the British Mandate, whose land law was claimed to 'embrace the system of tenures inherited from the Ottoman regime *enriched by amendments* [our italics], mostly of a declaratory character, enacted since the British occupation, on the authority of the Palestine Order-in-Council 1922-40' (Survey 1946-7: 225). Among the first actions of the occupying British were to close the Ottoman land registers, prohibit all land transactions until a new registry was installed, and transfer much jurisdiction in land matters from Islamic *shari'a* courts to new secular land courts. Two Mandate lawyers prepared 'as comprehensive a treatise on the Land Law of Palestine as is possible in the present circumstances' (Goadby and Doukhan 1935), and the resulting book has been called 'a master-piece of how colonial regimes occupy legal systems' (Strawson 2002: 370).

The Mandate recognised the five land tenure types in Ottoman law (Goadby & Doukhan 1935), which were as follows:

> *Mulk land* (fully-owned urban freehold property). The 7 per cent of the land of Israel still in private ownership is mostly former *mulk* land, mostly located within Arab villages.
>
> *Miri* land. This had heritable use rights, but could revert to the state if not cultivated after three years (*mahlul*), and then be auctioned to anyone prepared to cultivate it. *Miri* land represented the largest proportion of land in Palestine, and after 1948 was mostly acquired by the Israeli state, particularly through strict application of the three-year rule.
>
> State land required for public purposes (*matruka*, meaning withdrawn) and registered with the state or local authority. This included military bases, roads, forest land. and public open spaces within villages.

> Dead land (*mawat*), ie uncultivated, un-irrigated and vacant land, needing government consent to bring it into cultivation. Islamic law defined 'dead land' as sufficiently far from an inhabited place (a distance regarded as in practice a mile and a half) that a human voice could not be heard. *Mawat* in Palestine included the Negev desert and the 3000 sq.km. of mountain and desert east of Hebron, Jerusalem & Nablus. Article 6 of the League of Nations Mandate made it and *matruka* land available for Jewish settlement.
>
> *Waqf* land, held in trust for Muslim religious and charitable purposes. In 1948 *waqf* land was estimated to comprise a sixth of the country (Dumper 1994), and the Palestinians' culture of the sacred *waqf* is reflected in their treatment of *waqf* plots, often olive groves, which were cultivated by community volunteers, who would afterwards meticulously clean from their clothes traces of the sacred *waqf* soil.

During the Mandate period the British established a Supreme Muslim Council in 1921, which managed *shari'a* affairs in Palestine. Its *waqf* activities from 1921 to 1936 were impressive:

> Twenty-one new mosques and three minarets built, and 313 mosques repaired (notably the *Al Aqsa* mosque in Jerusalem).
>
> 224 new properties built, and 300 repaired, including shops, houses, and the *waqf* building (originally the Palace Hotel in Jerusalem, after 1948 used as Government offices).
>
> Draining of swamps, Planting of trees on *waqf* lands, and enlargement of *waqf* lands by the purchase of about 25,000 dunums.
>
> Maintenance of schools and award of scholarships for Muslim students to universities in Egypt, Syria, and Europe.
>
> Establishment of a Moslem orphanage, training of midwives. (Survey 1946-47)

After 1948 the new Israeli state reformulated regulations which had been devised in 1939 by the British for wartime conditions, as the 1949 Emergency Regulations on Property of Absentees, subsequently the Absentees Property Law 1950. A Custodian of Absentee Property was instituted, similar to the preceding Mandate Custodian of Enemy Property. Property abandoned by Arab refugees passed into the control of the new Israeli administration, with the confiscation of two million *dunams* to the Custodian, who later transferred the land to the development authority. Land in *waqf* ownership also passed from Muslim hands to the Custodian, since Israel did not distinguish between *waqf* property and other land, and the Custodian of Absentee Property claimed *waqf* property on the ground that the Supreme Muslim Council had become an 'absentee' (most of its members becoming refugees in 1948). Thus the Custodian was a conduit through which land passed to the Israeli Development Authority, and later the Israel Land Authority, in effect as a means of 'laundering' confiscated Palestinian land. The Absentee Law 1950 prohibited the *shari'a* court from supervising *waqf* property, while the Israeli high court held, in *Habab v the Custodian over Absentee Property (58/54)* that the custodian was neither a trustee of the properties, nor responsible for their management; also the absentee was not entitled to take legal action against the custodian (Jiryis 1981: 84)

Another modification of Mandate emergency regulations was the Emergency Regulations (Cultivation of Waste Lands) Law, 5709-1949. This law derived legitimacy not only from Mandate law but also the Ottoman Land Code, which had provided for special commissions to record abandoned villages and reclassify vacant land lying idle and 'exposed to the sun' (*shamsieh*) as state domain. It empowered the Ministry of Agriculture to declare lands as 'waste' lands (Article 2), and to take control of 'uncultivated' lands (Article 4), which could be confiscated without having to confirm the absentee status of owners. Much of the land abandoned by the Palestinians in 1948 was not recorded in the Ottoman or Mandate land registers, as many did not register their land for fear of tax collectors and military conscription. While much urban property was held freehold (*mulk*), agricultural land was classed as *miri,* in which formal and ultimate ownership was held by the State, and which if uncultivated for three years could be reclaimed by the state (COHRE & Badil 2005).

A further important law for land confiscation was the so-called 1965 amendment, described by Israeli scholars as a 'reform' of the *waqf* in Israel: the Absentees' Property (Amendment No. 3) (Release and Use of Endowment Property) Law

1965. The Board of Trustees of the Muslim *awqaf* was made up of government appointees, who would sell or exchange land with the ILA unaccountable to the Muslim community, and this sometimes caused violence within the Palestinian community, including assassinations. The 1965 amendment represented a further stage in the confiscation by authorising the transfer of *waqf* property to the Custodian, denying the conditions that were attached when the property was endowed, and ensuring that property confiscated from the *waqf* would not be returned, regardless of whether the *mutawalli* or the beneficiary is classed as an 'absentee'. The law empowered the Custodian to pass the property to the Development Authority or to a board of trustees, ostensibly to prevent its neglect, but in practice to sell it for development, contradicting the fundamental perpetual characteristic of *waqf* land. It freed the remaining *waqf* from restrictions under *shari'a* law, and also restricted the political use of funds generated from those *awqaf*. The state thus acquired a further tool to transfer remaining *waqf* properties from Muslim hands to the Jewish community through the use of Muslim 'state appointees' to a board of trustees (Dumper 1994).

Waqf Land in Jerusalem: Special Status

The situation with *waqf* property is particularly complicated in Jerusalem, because of that city's special status under international law, and it comprises some 90 percent of property within the Old City (both Islamic and Christian). Jordan continues to exercise its sovereignty and law over *waqf* institutions in Jerusalem through the Ministry of Waqf in Amman, and, while Jordanian law became obsolete with the establishment of the Palestinian Authority (PA) in the West Bank and Gaza, it still forms the legal basis for some institutions in Jerusalem where the PA is not allowed to function. During the Mandate the Palestinians used *waqf* properties as a buffer against the sale of land to the Jews. Jordanian control during the 19 years of its rule (1948-67) allowed the decline of *waqf*, with only 16 new *awqaf* being founded in Jerusalem, compared with 90 under the first 23 years of Israeli occupation (1967-1990) (Reiter 1996). Israel maintained the sovereignty of Muslim institutions and the *waqf* in East Jerusalem (including the Old City). Individual *waqf* property is recorded in the *Shari'a* Court in Jerusalem and in the Department of Islamic *Awaqf*, but the extent of *waqf* property in the Old City is not publicly available.

Many Jerusalem residents rent from *waqf* institutions. Since 1967 rents agreed under Jordanian rule are not recognised by Israeli law, and have not increased in line with inflation, resulting in dilapidation of much *waqf* property in the Old City (Lapidoth 1995). Cases decided by the *Shari'a* Court in East Jerusalem on rent or tenancy issues could only be enforced by the civil courts, which are Israeli and so not recognised by the *Shari'a* Court. The *mutawalli* of family *waqf* cannot resolve *waqf* property disputes, because a Palestinian court decision cannot be enforced, and will not take action in the Israeli *shari'a* court because this would be recognizing its jurisdiction over Jerusalem. As a result of this 'void in legal authority', the family *waqf* managers and the Administration have had to rely on moral and community pressure to enforce decisions. Investment in property and establishing new *awqaf* were neglected as a result of the uncertainty and the ambiguity. leading to property blight in Jerusalem particularly in the Old City (Dumper 1994: 111).

The Tenancy Protection Act of 1954 provides that a tenant cannot be evicted either for non-payment of rent, alterations, or sub-letting if resident for more than fifteen years. Additionally most leases allow a tenant to sub-let with *mutawalli* having no control over the sub-letting but still responsible for upkeep. Rent increases were linked to the cost of living index, but only for rents charged in Israeli shekels, while most properties in the Old City are charged in Jordanian dinars, and tenants can avoid rent increases with support from Israeli courts. Some landlords changed rents to Israeli shekels, seen as more stable than Jordanian, but deflation of the Israeli currency devalued these rents, while Israeli law prohibits lease revisions or eviction of tenants (Qupty 1998: 15–16). Commercial and cultural activities could flourish with Palestinians avoiding full landlord or Israeli control, but investment and development were neglected because of legal uncertainties and ambiguities, as the field-work revealed. In a study of the *awqaf* of six families in Jerusalem and reading 100 *waqf* deeds, Al-Alami (2006: 147-153) found that the long-term control of these *awqaf* by families gave them special benefits such as long-term leases of valuable *waqf* assets. The Israeli district court issued an initial decision allowing itself the right to review cases related to Islamic *Waqf* property in Jerusalem, but with the potential to be applied all over Palestine.

Mosques and Graveyards as Sites of Resistance

The Absentee Property Laws precluded Muslims from protecting and maintaining their sacred places, and many were subsequently transferred by the custodian to the development authority, which sold on to Jewish investment companies, so that eventually many mosques and cemeteries became museums, cafes, restaurants or even synagogues. The remaining unsold mosques are deserted, and cannot be maintained and used by Muslims who are denied access to them.

In 1951 the Ministry of Religious Affairs and the Custodian agreed that the ministry would be directly responsible for the management of sacred places, and this was confirmed by the government in 1952. The *Protection of Holy Places Law* 1967 (Article 1) states that:

> The Holy Places shall be protected from destruction and any other violation and from anything likely to violate the freedom of access of the members of different religions to the places sacred to them or their feelings with regard to those places.

This guarantee was inserted to neutralize international public opinion, but there was no clear definition of "sacred place" in the Israeli legal system (Berkovits 2006). Adjudication is still governed by a 1924 Mandate law, upheld by the Israel Supreme Court, with matters relating to religious rights in the Holy Places (including disputes between denominations of the same religion, and between religions) decided by the government, not adjudicated in the courts.

About a third of Muslim *waqf* property, principally mosques and graveyards still in use, was not expropriated after 1948, and in the early 1990s, following the Oslo accords, the Islamic Movement in Israel started to survey the *waqf* properties, intending to protect and develop them, and to prevent attempts by Israeli authorities to change their status and sell them off through the state-appointed trustees. Various cases illustrate the progress (or lack of it) of that contestation, as investigated in the field research for this article.

Among the disputes over waqf properties was that involving the Muslim cemetery of Haifa, *Jamia' al-estiqlal,* used since the Mandate. In 1993 the *shari'a* court in Haifa confirmed an agreement between two *mutawallis* and an Israeli company regarding a deal to develop the site, but some months later one of the signatory *mutawallis* applied to the *shari'a* court to cancel the agreement, since the same *qadi* Zaki Midlij who permitted the agreement disowned it. The *mutawalli* then applied to the High Court, relying on an additional statement of *qadi* Midlij, in which he claimed he had been coerced under armed threat from the company's lawyer. The police questioned the *qadi,* who resigned over the matter as a *qadi* of the *shari'a* court of appeal. The two parties agreed to transfer the case to the civil court in Haifa, where it is still pending.

The Adalah organisation (the Legal Centre for Arab Minority Rights in Israel) petitioned the Supreme Court in the name of Muslim religious leaders to demand legal recognition for the Muslim Holy Places in Israel. A special committee was formed in 2000, to investigate the situation of Arab holy sites, with representation from the Ministry of Religious Affairs, the Ministry of National Infrastructures, the Israel Lands Administration, and the Regional Committee for Arab Local Councils. The committee prepared a plan for abandoned non-Jewish holy sites, compiling a list of 53 Muslim holy sites and 58 abandoned Muslim cemeteries, but the Ministry of Religious Affairs did not implement the committee's recommendations. In *Bhmr 1931/97* the Israeli civil court held that a mosque should be considered as a sacred place only if the property itself is sacred (the use in itself being insufficient). In Islamic law, however, a *shari'a* court *qadi* can confirm the sacred element: mosques and graveyards remained sacred, even without a roof.

The *qadi* of the *shari'a* Court of Appeal Ahmed *Natur* issued a *marsoom qadai* (legal decree), legally binding on all *shari'a qadis*, which attempted a tougher line. With the Muslim *waqf* places, and the sacred places specifically, gradually losing their status, abuse of *waqf* properties had become a routine practice, with manipulation of the *shari'a* courts to secure their release to Israeli control. The *qadi*'s *marsoom*, for the 'public benefit' of Muslims in accordance with Islamic law, criticised the Israeli state for confiscating *awqaf* properties, and proposed procedural steps to protect the remaining *awqaf* from extinction. The *shari'a qadis* were not allowed to deliver any *fatwa* which might permit the use of sacred *waqf* properties or any other *awqaf*, for other purposes than those declared in the *waqfiya*. Even if the *qadi* tried to rely upon *shari'a* judgments, they might violate basic principles. Mosques were declared sacred even when closed or deserted, 'as long as one prayer was performed there'. The *qadi* could not issue or confirm agreements on *waqf* property when these effected sale, rent, or substitution. *Shari'a* courts appointing *mutawallis* should call them to account every six months, with reports kept in an official register available to the public (an important procedure as previously many *fatwas* and approvals were inadequately documented). The *shari'a* courts should dismiss *mutawalli* who abused their positions and took no action to protect the *waqf*. The *shari'a* courts were not allowed to appoint *mutawallis* without permission of the *shari'a* court of appeal, choosing only those who had good character, history and no criminal record. The Israeli Minister of Religious Affairs, however, by letter of 3 June 1996 rejected the *marsoom,* claiming that *qadi Natour* was not authorised to issue it. *Qadi*

Natour challenged the minister as improperly intervening in the judicial system, arguing that the *shari'a* Court of Appeal had jurisdiction.

The case of the Beer el-Sabe (Beersheva) 'big mosque' further illustrates the conflict over *waqf*. The first mosque in the Naqab (Negev), it was founded in 1906, with Arab Bedouin sheikhs contributing half of the funding. After 1948 the mosque was confiscated, and was used as a court and prison until 1953, then as a museum until 1991, but has since been neglected and unprotected, surrounded by restaurants and bars, a municipal building and a public garden. In 2005, the Supreme Court of Israel sat to adjudicate on a petition submitted by *Adalah,* the Legal Centre for Arab Minority Rights in Israel. In 2002, a request was made for the re-opening of the Big Mosque for Muslim prayer. At the time Beer el-Sabe had some 259 synagogues for 180,000 Jewish residents (one for every 700), while the 5,000 Muslim residents had no mosque, not to mention the 150,000 Muslims in the surrounding Naqab. The petition was submitted by *Adalah* on behalf of the Association for Support and Defence of Bedouin Rights in Israel, the Islamic Committee in the Naqab, and 23 Palestinian citizens of Israel, against the Municipality of Beer el-Sabe, the Development Authority, the Ministry of Religious Affairs, and the Minister of Science. *Adalah* argued that free access to the mosque was protected by the right to freedom of religion. The Israeli police force claimed that reinstating the mosque would create inter-community conflict, and the municipality argued that it would bring the ownership of all Muslim religious sites into dispute, even the Temple Mount and Jerusalem. *Adalah* argued that maintaining the *status quo* would continue discrimination against Muslims, violating the right of freedom of worship. *Adalah* added that "there was no presence or representation of any Muslims from Beer el-Sabe or elsewhere on the Committee, and that, as it was formed by and constituted of members of various governmental offices, who are essentially a party to the dispute with an interest in maintaining the *status quo*, the Committee's recommendations were neither just nor objective" (Adallah 2005: 4). Justices Procaccia, Hayut and Jubran ordered that the parties review their positions and within sixty days reach an agreement to convert the mosque to a cultural and social centre for use by the Muslim community of Beer el-Sabe, *except for the purpose of praying*. In 2009 the Supreme Court upheld the previous decisions, still denying Muslims use of the building for prayer.

In the case *2289/81,* involving the *waqf Alestiqlal* cemetery *in Haifa,* the Muslim community in Haifa petitioned in the district court to prevent the *mutawallis* transferring the bones of the Muslim dead elsewhere, and to develop the site. The court claimed that it had no jurisdiction, but referred the case to the *shari'a* court, which allowed the transfer, asserting that the sacredness of a cemetery lapses after 36 years of abandonment. Similar approaches have been adopted in other cases. In *232/76 (Shukri v Sharia Court-Bagats)*, the court upheld and reiterated the *Alestiqlal* judgment. The *qadi* Tawfiq Asaliya in 1969 had stated that after 36 years the status of the *Salma* cemetery in Jaffa changed to 'outworn', but he reversed that decision in 1991, then claiming that 'the sacredness of graveyards is eternal and this entitlement cannot be nullified as it belongs to Allah', so no-one should destroy graves there.

The *Ijzim* cemetery raised similar issues recently, resulting in Palestinian demonstrations on site. In 1949, a Jewish settlement was built on the lands of the Palestinian village *Ijzim,* whose inhabitants fled after the 1948 war. In 2002 Jewish developers bought land which included a graveyard of Muslim and Christian Palestinians. In 2004 the *'Al-Aqsa* institution for the development of *waqf* properties applied to the Israeli Supreme Court to stop construction work, because of the destruction of Muslim graves. The appeal relied upon the 2004 fatwa of *qadi* Ahmed Natour, stating that:

> the sacredness of graveyards is eternal and no one is permitted to remove it... insulting graves and the cemetery for the purpose of building a residential area as in this case is forbidden.... the landscape of the graveyard (even though it was not used for long time) is still considered as *waqf* and it cannot be confiscated, nor it can be used for other purposes [translated from Arabic].

The developers disputed that the land was a cemetery, arguing that the graveyard recognised by the authorities was at some distance, and that local Muslims did not regard it as such, but admitted that graves had been discovered on the site, and the Ministry of Religious Affairs barred them from removal. In 2009, however, the Supreme Court rejected the petition and allowed construction to continue.

The *Maamano-Allah* Graveyard in West Jerusalem has been another recent case. Dating from at least the 13th century (Muslim tradition claims that companions of the Prophet Muhammad are buried there), the cemetery was declared absentee property in 1955 (although there was no publicity in Arabic as required under Israeli law), and during the next 30 years the municipality of Jerusalem gradually acquired ownership, with objections being filed but over-ruled. In 2004 the Simon Wiesenthal Centre began constructing a Museum of Tolerance on part of the cemetery, with a much-publicized ground-breaking ceremony attended by California Governor Arnold Schwarzenegger, the Israeli President and Vice Prime Minister, the Mayor of Jerusalem, and dignitaries and guests from around the world. The centre aims to 'fortify the value of tolerance between peoples and between man to man'. When work uncovered human graves, the *Al-Aqsa* institution petitioned the Supreme Court for a provisional injunction preventing construction, and the dispute was brought to the *shari'a* and civil courts, who issued conflicting judgments. In 2009 the Israeli Supreme Court confirmed that three Muslim cemeteries (*Maamano-Allah*, *Ijzim* and *Alberwa*) could be confiscated to Jewish developers, against Palestinian objections which included demonstrations on site.

Conclusions: 'into a dark tunnel'

The British Mandate over Palestine legislated for an array of modern land management tools, and allowed the mutation of the despised but useful Ottoman/Islamic land law for Israeli purposes, retaining a religious communal basis which could be pre-empted. The state of Israel came into existence in 1948 as the inheritor of a body of non-Jewish law derived from Ottoman law, following a positivist ideology of law and the state. Having driven out most of the Palestinians, it then modified the Mandate institution of the Custodian of Enemy Property, designed to hold such property in trust pending the end of hostilities, into the Custodian of Absentee Property, drawing upon the legal concept of 'absentee' in the Ottoman Land Code. The new state already had control of state and waste land, transferred to it by the outgoing Mandate administration, and used its powers against absentee property to confiscate large tracts of land. It treated *waqf* land as little different from other absentee property, disregarding the perpetuity element conferred under *shari'a* law, although 'holy' and 'sacred' places were placed under special protection, and there were particular arrangements for the Old City of Jerusalem. Palestinian attempts since the 1990s to revive *waqf* status and protect mosques and cemeteries from confiscation and change of use have generally been denied in Israeli courts, with *shari'a* court judgments over-ruled. As expressed by the director of *Awqaf* in Jerusalem, petitioning the Israeli court is 'like walking into a dark tunnel. Nobody can tell what is waiting for him at the other end'.

With the culture of endowing new *awqaf* disappearing under Israeli disapproval (except in Jerusalem), the role of *waqf* property in social and economic development has not been realised for Palestinian society, although it is being rediscovered in many Muslim countries after a century of stagnation. The Israeli state did not incorporate *waqf-khayri* into the state structure as other Arab countries have done, but confiscated *awqaf,* denied Muslim jurisdiction over them and deprived the Muslim community from benefiting from them.

References

AKGUNDFIZ, A.
1996 *Islam Hukukunda ve Osmanl Tatbikatznda Vakzf Miies-sesesi, 2nd* Istanbul, Turkey: OSAV [in Turkish].
AL QARADAWI, Y.
1976 "*Al Iman wa Al Hayat*", [Faith and Life], Beirut: Mu'sassat Al Risalah [in Arabic].
BAER, G.
1990 'The dismemberment of awqaf in early 19th century Jerusalem.' Pp.299-319 in: G. G. Gilbar (ed.), *Ottoman Palestine 1800–1914: Studies in Economic and Social History*, Leiden: E. J. Brill.
BAGAEEN, Samer
2006 'Evaluating the Effects of Ownership and Use on the Condition of Property in the Old City of Jerusalem.' *Housing Studies* 21: 135-50
BERKOVITS, Shmuel
2006 *How dreadful is this Place: Holiness, Politics and Justice in Jerusalem and the Holy Places in Israel*, Jerusalem: *Carta Jerusalem* [in Hebrew].
BLOMLEY, Nicholas, D. Delaney, et al.
2001 *The Legal Geographies Reader*. Oxford: Blackwell.
COHRE (Centre on Housing Rights and Evictions) & BADIL (Resource Centre for Palestinian Residents and Refugee Rights)
2005 *Ruling Palestine, A History of the Legally Sanctioned Jewish-Israeli Seizure of Land and Housing in Palestine* May Publishers [available online at badil.com]
DUMPER, Michael
1994 *Islam and Israel: Muslim Religious Endowments and the Jewish State* Washington, D.C.: Institute for Palestine Studies.
GAUDIOSI, Monica
1988 'The influence of the Islamic Law of Waqf on the Development of the Trust in England: The Case of Merton College.' *University of Pennsylvania Law Review* 136: 1231-61.

GOADBY, Frederick and Moses DOUKHAN

1935 *The Land Law of Palestine*. Jerusalem: Government (reprinted 1998 by Gaunt, Holmes Beach, Florida).

HENNIGAN, P. C.

2004 *The Birth of a Legal Institution: The Formation of the Waqf in Third-Century A.H. Hanafi Legal Discourse*. London: Brill.

HOME, Robert

2003 'An Irreversible Conquest? Colonial and Postcolonial Land Law in Israel/Palestine.' *Social & Legal Studies* 12: 291-310.

HUSSEIN, Hussein Ali and Fiona McKAY.

2003 *Access Denied: Palestinian Land Rights in Israel* London: Zed Books

JIRYIS, Sabri

1981 'Domination by the Law.' *Journal of Palestine Studies* 11: 67-92

KAHF, Monzer

1999 'Towards the Revival of *Awqaf*: A Few *Fiqhi* Issues to Reconsider', Paper presented to Harvard Forum on Islamic Finance and Economics.

KAMINKER, Sarah

1997 'For Arabs only: building restrictions in East Jerusalem.' *Journal of Palestine Studies* 26: 5–16.

KEDAR, Sandy (Alexandre)

2001 'The legal transformation of ethnic geography: Israel law and the Palestinian landholder 1948-1967.' *Journal of International Law and Politics* 33: 923-1000.

KURAN, Timur

2001 'The Provision of Public Goods under Islamic Law: Origins, Impact, and Limitation of the Waqf System', *Law and Society Review* 35: 841-97

2004 'Why the Middle East is Economically Underdeveloped: Historical Mechanisms of Institutional Stagnation.' *Journal of Economic Perspectives* 18: 71-90.

LAPIDOTH, Ruth

1995 *Whither Jerusalem? Proposals and Positions Concerning the Future of Jerusalem* The Hague: Kluwer Law.

LAYISH, Aharon

1997 'The Family *Waqf* and the *Shari'a* Law of Succession in Modern Times.' *Islamic Law and Society* 4: 352-388.

LEEUWEN, Richard van

1999 *Waqfs and Urban Structures: The Case of Ottoman Damascus*, Leiden: Brill.

MORRIS, Benny
2000 *Righteous Victims: A History of the Zionist-Arab Conflict 1881-1999* London: John Murray.

PETERS, Francis
1986 *Jerusalem and Mecca: The Typology of the Holy City in the Near East*, New York: University Press.

QUPTY, Mazen
1998 "The legal situation of property in the Old City and its implications for its restoration". paper presented to the Welfare Association.

REITER, Yitzhak
1996 *Islamic Endowments in Jerusalem under British Mandate* London: Frank Cass.

SAIT, Siraj and Hilary LIM
2006 *Land, Law & Islam: Property and Human Rights in the Muslim World* London: Zed Books.

SAYED, A. M
1989 'Role of Awqaf in Islamic History", in Hassan Abdullah Al Amin (ed.), *Idarat Wa Tathmir Mumtalakat Al Awqaf*, IRTI, Jeddah [in Arabic].

SHAMIR, Ronen
2000 *The Colonies of Law: Colonialism, Zionism and Law in Early Mandate Palestine*. Cambridge, University Press.

STRAWSON, John.
2002 'Reflections on Edward Said and the legal narratives of Palestine: Israeli settlements and Palestinian self-determination', *Penn State International Law Review* 20: 363-384.

SURVEY
1946-47 *A Survey of Palestine* (3 vols.). Washington: Anglo-American Committee (reprinted 1991 by Institute for Palestine Studies).

YEDIYILDIZ, B.
1985 *Institution du Vaqf au XVIIIe Siecle en Turqui:* Ankara, Turkey: Editions Ministere de la Culture.

ZARQA, Muhammed Anas
1994 'Financing and Investment in Awqaf Projects: A non Technical Introduction.' *Islamic Economic Studies* I: 55-62.

DISTINCTION WITHOUT DIFFERENCE: THE CONSTITUTIONAL PROTECTION OF CUSTOMARY LAW AND CULTURAL, LINGUISTIC AND RELIGIOUS COMMUNITIES - A COMMENT ON *SHILUBANA AND OTHERS v. NWAMITWA*

E.S. Nwauche

Introduction

Even though the decision of the South African Constitutional Court (the CC) in *Shilubana and Others v Nwamitwa* ([2008] ZACC 9 (CC), the *Shilubana* case) is commendable because "it promotes gender equality in the succession of traditional leadership, in accordance with the Constitution" (para. 1; for comments on this case see Mmusinyane 2009), this comment is primarily concerned with how the CC deferred to communal norms ordered by the Valoyi Tribe through its customary law. Furthermore even though the *Shilubana* case appears to herald a more sympathetic understanding of customary law, it also reveals the fact that customary law applies exclusively to the black community in South Africa while other racial communities are imagined and protected in terms of sections 30[1] and 31[2] of the Constitution of the Republic of South Africa 1996 (the Final Constitution, FC[3]). It is the contention of this paper that this distinction is not only wrong but of no significant difference. It is further contended that protection of all racial communities should proceed on the basis of sections 30 and 31 of the FC because the framework of these two sections appears better suited for the protection of all communities if South African courts show a more sympathetic understanding of communal norms and institutions. This comment argues that the *Shilubana* case is a tentative but welcome example of this trend. In the case the CC upheld a decision of the Valoyi Tribe to appoint a woman as a traditional leader. This was a development of its customary law of traditional succession that had hitherto operated on the basis of male primogeniture. In accepting this development the CC did not question the manner of the developed traditional succession even though it was open to the Court either to abolish the traditional institution of chieftaincy or on the basis of the right to equality[4] to declare that it

---

[1] 30. Everyone has the right to use the language and to participate in the cultural life of their choice, but no one exercising these rights may do so in a manner inconsistent with any provision of the Bill of Rights.

[2] 31. (1) Persons belonging to a cultural, religious or linguistic community may not be denied the right, with other members of that community

(a) to enjoy their culture, practise their religion and use their language; and

(b) to form, join and maintain cultural, religious and linguistic associations and other organs of civil society.

(2) The rights in subsection (1) may not be exercised in a manner inconsistent with any provision of the Bill of Rights.

[3] Part of the unique transition of South Africa included the adoption of an Interim Constitution in 1993 and a Final Constitution in 1996.

[4] Section 9 of the FC provides:

(1) Everyone is equal before the law and has the right to equal protection and benefit of the law.

(2) Equality includes the full and equal enjoyment of all rights and freedoms. To promote the achievement of equality, legislative and other measures designed to protect or advance

was an elective position to be filled by universal adult suffrage. In recognizing a gender neutral traditional leadership institution, the Court demonstrated that institutions established by communal norms can exist and function on the basis of equality and other rights which are the hallmarks of a liberal constitution.

This comment is organized as follows. The next part undertakes a brief overview of group rights in the FC. Part three considers the exclusive association of customary law with the 'black' community and whether this association has enhanced the group rights of the black community. In part four, the comment undertakes an assessment of the interpretation of the rights of members of cultural, linguistic and religious communities to ascertain how far they advance group rights. Part five in concluding remarks urges a unified interpretation of 'communities' and a more beneficial interpretation of 'group rights' that recognizes that all racial groups have a customary law and deserve a more sensitive recognition of their communal norms.

Group Rights in the Final Constitution

This comment adopts a definition of group rights as meaning those rights which are granted to cultural groups (Oomen 1999). Even though group rights appear to be of different categories (Levy 1997: 75-76), this comment is concerned with the recognition and enforcement of those rules and regulations formulated by social

persons, or categories of persons, disadvantaged by unfair discrimination may be taken.
(3) The state may not unfairly discriminate directly or indirectly against anyone on one or more grounds, including race, gender, sex, pregnancy, marital status, ethnic or social origin, colour, sexual orientation, age, disability, religion, conscience, belief, culture, language and birth.
(4) No person may unfairly discriminate directly or indirectly against anyone on one or more grounds in terms of subsection (3). National legislation must be enacted to prevent or prohibit unfair discrimination.
(5) Discrimination on one or more of the grounds listed in subsection (3) is unfair unless it is established that the discrimination is fair.

groups for members' conduct and enforced in a variety of ways. The purpose of this section is to identify any group rights in the FC. The protection offered by sections 30 and 31 of the FC[5] is an individual right by its cast. However this right may in certain circumstances also qualify albeit indirectly as a group right in the manner in which the right is exercised. In *Christian Education SA v Minister of Education of the Government of SA* (1999 2 SA 83 (CC), the *Christian Education* case) the nature of the right granted in section 31 is explained by Sachs J:

> The rights protected by section 31 are significant both for individuals and for the communities they constitute. If the community as community dies, whether through destruction or assimilation, there would be nothing left in respect of which the individual could exercise associational rights. Moreover, if society is to be open and democratic in the fullest sense it needs to be tolerant and accepting of cultural pluralism... the protection of diversity is not effected through giving legal personality to groups as such. It is achieved indirectly through the double mechanism of positively enabling individuals to join with other individuals of their community, and negatively enjoining the state not to deny them the rights collectively to profess and practise their own religion (as well as enjoy their culture and use their language). (1999 2 SA 83 (CC): para. 23)

It is thus possible that in the interpretation of sections 30 and 31 of the FC a court can choose whether to privilege community as against individual rights or to interpret communal rights through an individual prism. It appears that since the FC is a strong modern liberal constitution, an interpretation of communal rights from an individual perspective is inevitable.

The rights created by customary law have both an individual and a group dimension. On one hand it may be asserted that the constitutional recognition of customary law[6] approximates customary law as a group right because this recognition is a promise that the norms (of customary law) developed by (black)

---

[5] Above, notes 1, 2.

[6] FC, s. 211(3) provides that the courts must apply customary law when that law is applicable, subject to the Constitution and any legislation that specifically deals with customary law.

communities to order their lives will be recognized by the FC. On the other hand many will deny that the FC recognizes any group right and that a conscious effort was made to exclude substantive group recognition in the FC (Murray and Simeon 2007). On this score customary law can find justification in sections 30 and 31 of the FC (Bennett 2005) to the extent that individual members of (black) communities can urge a court to recognize their (communal) cultural religious or linguistic norms. Constitutional scrutiny of customary law, it follows, should proceed without much deference to the communal norms but with a keen eye to ensuring that individual rights are protected. It is this second reading that appears evident in the case of the FC.

It therefore can be summarized that in the protection offered by customary law and by sections 30 and 31 of the Final Constitution the individual interest appears to be superior to the community interest. This is not surprising since the FC is a modern liberal constitution with a strong individual ethos which the CC has on numerous occasions recognized.[7] It is therefore open to question not only whether group rights can be found in the FC but also what is the nature of these group rights. This comment proceeds in the next section to examine whether the communal dimension of customary law has been recognized in the constitutional protection of customary law in South Africa.

Is Customary Law only for the 'Black' Community? An Overview of the Recognition of Communal Interests in the Constitutional Protection of Customary Law

This section of the comment first determines whether customary law is by any interpretation reserved exclusively for the 'Black' community and then proceeds to determine how this interpretation affects the recognition of group rights. The recognition of customary law by the FC[8] is not accompanied by any definition of

[7] See for example: *President of the Republic of South Africa v Hugo* 1997 6 BCLR 708 (CC) para. 14; *National Coalition for Gay and Lesbian Equality v Minister of Justice* 1999 1 SA 6 (CC), para. 30.

[8] See sec 211(3). The CC has held:

> While in the past indigenous law was seen through the common law lens, it must now be seen as an integral part of our law. Like all law it depends for its ultimate force and validity on the

customary law nor does it textually associate customary law with the 'Black' community. The Recognition of Customary Marriages Act 1998 (the Recognition Act) however defines customary law as "Customs and usages traditionally observed among indigenous African peoples and which form part of the culture of those peoples". This association of customary law with the 'black' community is also recognized by the judiciary in cases in which customary law has been in issue. For example in *Elizabeth Gumede v President South Africa and Others* ([2008] ZACC 23, the *Gumede* case) Moseneke DCJ wondered whether "people other than indigenous African people may be bound by customary law" ([2008] ZACC 23, para. 23). Academic opinion assumes the link between customary law and the black community (Pieterse 2001; Kaganas and Murray 1994). Overwhelming evidence therefore associates customary law with 'Black' people. There is however no evidence that the term is *exclusive* to them. In other words other peoples in South Africa can also have a 'customary law'. If the definition in the Recognition Act is acceptable and devoid of its racial association it would appear that the customs and usages observed by other peoples can also form the basis of 'white' or 'coloured' customary law. In fact the FC is commendable because it does not limit 'customary law' to the 'black' community. If the practice of the past is anything to go by, the recognition of customary law as applying only to blacks was an assertion of the legal system that other races had no normative system outside the dominant English Common law and Roman-Dutch Law. Social practice, I think, shows otherwise.

There are a number of issues that are important in the constitutional recognition of customary law, including the ascertainment and proof of customary law (Himonga and Bosch 2000; Bennett 2009), that deserve further examination because of the *Shilubana* case. However, the remaining part of this section dwells only on two issues that illustrate the focus of this paper and further justify the assertion that customary law should not be restricted to only the black community. The first is the scope of 'black' customary law while the second is the dominant ethos of customary law as it appears from recent cases. With respect to the first issue

---

> Constitution. Its validity must now be determined by reference not to common law, but to the Constitution. (*Alexkor Ltd and Another v Richtersveld Community and Others,* 2003 12 BCLR 1301 (CC), para. 51.)

See also *Mabuza v Mbatha* 2003 (4) SA 218 (C); 2003 7 BCLR 743 (C) at para. 32.

attention is drawn to the fact that the content of customary law generated by colonialism and domination is generally restricted to the private and personal, including land because of the critical manner in which land constitutes the private economic realm of members of communities subject to customary law. The obliteration of customary public law was fundamental to the task of subjugating colonized and dominated people. All through Africa, this was one of the important consequences of colonialism. This fact is so total that there is an instinctive association of customary law with personal law - inheritance, succession, marriage, and in certain circumstances chieftancy, customary land tenure and civil wrongs. Furthermore academic literature in South Africa assumes this fact (e.g. Rautenbach 2003; Lehnert 2005). If it is true that the *Shilubana* case is an example of significant deference to communal norms, one of the attendant questions is whether this deference will apply to all facets of customary norm making, public and private. To restrict customary law to the personal and private is to read the FC wrongly. If customary law is what is recognized it must be the whole of that system, again subject to the FC. Disassociating customary law from the 'black' community assists in a significant way in our recognition of how social practices of *all* communities in *all* spheres of endeavor can become part of the legal system.

The next issue is whether the judicial interpretation of the constitutional recognition of customary law reveals a sensitive understanding and recognition of communal interests. The majority judgment of the CC in *Bhe v Magistrate Khayelitsha and Others* (2005 1 BCLR 1 (CC), the *Bhe* case) will assist in this evaluation. The *Bhe* case evaluated the constitutionality of the customary law rule of male primogeniture. The Court held that the rule of male primogeniture was discriminatory and contravened the right to equality contained in section 9(3) and the right to dignity protected by section 10 of the FC, because women (widows and daughters) and extra-marital children were not allowed to participate in the intestate succession of deceased estates. The Court was faced with the problem of deciding what line of action to adopt in the light of this finding. According to Langa DCJ:

> In considering an appropriate remedy in this case, various courses present themselves. They are: (a) whether the Court should simply strike the impugned provisions down and leave it to the legislature to deal with the gap that would result as it sees fit; (b) whether to suspend the declaration of invalidity of the impugned provisions for a specified period; (c) whether the customary law rules of succession should be developed in

> accordance with the "spirit, purport and objects of the Bill of Rights", or (d) whether to replace the impugned provisions with a modified section 1 of the Intestate Succession Act or with some other order. (2005 1 BCLR 1 (CC), para. 105; footnotes omitted.)

The Court chose to follow option 'd' and modified the Intestate Succession Act which provided for succession to the deceased estate by a surviving spouse. The modification to the Act sought to protect partners to monogamous and polygamous customary marriages as well as unmarried women and their respective children. This was to be an interim measure until Parliament enacts a comprehensive regime.

The majority judgment declined to develop the customary law of succession because it felt that this would depend on a case by case development which would be slow and that the uncertainties regarding the rules of customary law would be prolonged (2005 1 BCLR 1 (CC), paras. 111 and 112). The various options considered by the majority judgment are actually a sub-set of one of the two options evident from the judgment, which were either to retain the customary law of succession or to dispense with it. In choosing the Intestate Succession Act, the majority judgment recognised that this could lead to the obliteration of the customary law of succession. If the majority had been minded otherwise, the Court could have proceeded to declare a rule that would give effect to the modified version of the Intestate Succession Act and in addition affirm the concomitant responsibilities of inheritance recognised by customary law. Accordingly surviving spouses and daughters would then inherit the property as heads of family and thereby create family property. The other option was to simply stop the discrimination against women and children and thereby develop the customary law of succession to bring it in line with the rights in the Bill of Rights until comprehensive legislation was enacted. This was an option explored and adopted by the minority judgment of Ngcobo J. which ensures that the concept of family property survives as a key aspect of a communal normative system while satisfying the demands of a modern liberal constitution.[9] The majority and minority

---

9 The defect in the rule of male primogeniture is that it excludes women from being considered for succession to the deceased family head. In this regard it deviates from section 9(3) of the Constitution. It needs to be developed so as to bring it in line with our Bill of Rights. This can be achieved by removing the

judgments are contrasting examples of what can befall customary law in a modern liberal Constitution. The majority judgment clearly sought to concentrate on the individual while the minority judgment also sought to protect the individual but within norms developed by the community for its survival and vitality. On a confrontation between the individual ethos of the Intestate Succession Act and the communal norms of customary law the latter lost out.

To sum up this part, it can be said that, even if South African courts adopt a more sympathetic understanding of customary law, the result could be the continuance of the many customary laws in South Africa, which appears untidy and undesirable. It is the contention of this paper that communities in South Africa will be better protected by the framework that is established by section 30 and 31 of the FC. It is to that framework that the paper turns to.

An Overview of the Constitutional Protection of Cultural, Linguistic and Religious Communities

In this section this paper sketches a broad overview of the constitutional protection of cultural, linguistic and religious communities in order to assess whether the nature of their protection significantly differs from the protection offered by customary law to 'black' communities. To locate the ensuing discussion in the context of the *Shilubana* case, this part concerns the manner in which the assertion of the internal norms of a cultural, linguistic and religious community have been evaluated and recognised. For many reasons, including space, this comment considers only the protection of religious communities.[10] Religious communities

reference to a male so as to allow an eldest daughter to succeed to the deceased estate. (2005 1 BCLR 1 (CC), para. 222.)

[10] Although South African constitutional jurisprudence is engaging with these issues, there are no discussions of the manner in which language rights have played out in South Africa. See the following cases: *Matukane v Laerskool Potgietersrus* 1996 3 SA 223 (T), *High School Ermelo and Anor v The Head of Department: Mpumalanga Department of Education and Others* [2007] ZAGPHC 232 (TPD); Case No 3062/2007 decided 17 October 2007; *Seodin Primary School and Others v MEC of Education, Northern Cape and Others* [2006] 1 All SA 154 (NC); *Laerskool Middleburg en 'n Ander v Departementshoof Mpumalanga Departement van Onderwys, en Andere* 2003 (4) SA 160 (T) 175; *Western Cape*

appear for now to be more involved than others in seeking recognition of their norms. This may not be surprising since religious identity is often fundamental in defining social groups. In general the discussion in this part will show that South African courts have generally not shown enough sensitivity to religious communities, although there are exceptions in certain cases where South African courts have recognized religious communal norms.

Three cases decided by the CC will be used to illustrate the unsympathetic posture of South African courts to religious communal norms. The first is the *Christian Education* case. The facts of this were that a voluntary association, which was an umbrella body of 196 independent Christian schools in South Africa with a total of approximately 14,500 pupils and with the aim "to promote evangelical Christian education", challenged the South African Schools Act which prohibited corporal punishment. The Association averred that its member schools maintained an active Christian ethos and sought to provide their learners an environment that was in keeping with their Christian faith. It further averred that corporal punishment was an integral part of this ethos and that the blanket prohibition of its use in its schools invaded their individual, parental and *community* rights to freely practise their religion. The Court held that the prohibition of corporal punishment was a justifiable limitation on the exercise of the individual parental and community rights of the appellants. The Court was satisfied that the justification lay in the interest of the State in protecting pupils from degradation and indignity arising from corporal punishment.

If the *Christian Education* case appears understandable given the peculiar violent history of South Africa, the decision of the CC in *Prince v President of the Cape Law Society* (2001 2 BCLR 133 (CC), interim judgment; 2002 2 SA 794 (CC), final judgment, the *Prince* case) may have cast the Court as unwilling to substantively recognize communal religious norms. In that case, concerning the disqualification of a Rastafarian from processes leading to qualification to practice law in South Africa, it was contended that the prohibition of the use and possession of cannabis by section 4(b) of the Drugs Act was unconstitutional because there was no exemption for the use and possession of cannabis for religious purposes in furtherance of the right to freedom of religion, opinion and

---

Minister of Education and Others v The Governing Body of Mikro Primary School 2006 1 SA 1 (SCA). See the following academic works: Fleisch and Woolman 2007; Bray 2007.

belief protected by section 15 of the FC.[11] It appeared as common cause that the use possession and transportation of cannabis by the Rastafarian community to which Prince belonged was central to the Rastafarian religion, as it was used for healing, communion, ritual, sacred medicinal and culinary purposes. In the opinion of the Rastafarian community their religion would disappear if cannabis were declared illegal. It was contended on behalf of the State that the prohibition was a justifiable limitation on the constitutional rights of freedom of religion opinion and belief.[12] It was argued that an exemption for the Rastafarian

[11] The text reads:

> 15. (1) Everyone has the right to freedom of conscience, religion, thought, belief and opinion.
>
> (2) Religious observances may be conducted at state or state-aided institutions, provided that [continued]
>
> a. those observances follow rules made by the appropriate public authorities;
> b. they are conducted on an equitable basis; and
> c. attendance at them is free and voluntary.
>
> (3) a. This section does not prevent legislation recognising
> i. marriages concluded under any tradition, or a system of religious, personal or family law; or
> ii. systems of personal and family law under any tradition, or adhered to by persons professing a particular religion.
> b. Recognition in terms of paragraph (a) must be consistent with this section and the other provisions of the Constitution.

[12] The general limitation clause in the FC is found in section 36 which provides:

> (1) The rights in the Bill of Rights may be limited only in terms of law of general application to the extent that the limitation is reasonable and justifiable in an open and democratic society based on human dignity, equality and freedom, taking into account all relevant factors, including
>
> a. the nature of the right;
> b. the importance of the purpose of the limitation;

community was possible but not practicable for a number of reasons, including the difficulty in administering an exemption, the fact that the prohibition aided the war on drugs, and South Africa's international law obligations. The majority judgment agreed with the State. The minority judgment accepted the need for an exemption for Rastafarians on the other hand and argued for a reasonably administered government supervision of the use and possession of cannabis. The principle of reasonable accommodation canvassed in Ngcobo J's minority judgment required the State to bear an extra burden in circumstances in which there is a clash between the law and faith. As Sachs J noted in his judgment concurring with the minority, this principle should operate when the practices do not violate any part of the Bill of Rights (2002 2 SA 794 (CC), para. 149[13]).

The trend in interpreting communal/ group rights through an individual prism was also present in the majority judgment of the CC in *MEC Education Kwa Zulu Natal v Pillay* (2008 1 SA 474(CC), the *Pillay* case). This judgment looked to the sincerely but subjectively held individual views in order to determine a sincerely held religious/cultural norm (Langa DCJ, 2008 1 SA 474(CC), para. 87). O'Regan J in her dissent points correctly to the fact that, with respect to culture and associative religions, the question "...will not be whether the practice forms part of the sincerely held personal beliefs of an individual, but whether the practice is a practice pursued by a particular cultural community" (2008 1 SA 474(CC), para. 147).

> c. the nature and extent of the limitation;
> d. the relation between the limitation and its purpose; and
> e. less restrictive means to achieve the purpose.

[13] In fn 10 to this paragraph there is an enumeration of practices that violate the Bill of Rights by Sachs J:

> [H]uman sacrifice, the immolation of widows or the stoning of adulterers, violate the Bill of Rights and accordingly are not rendered immune to state action simply on the grounds that they are embedded in religious belief. The sacramental use of dagga on the other hand comes nowhere near to infringing the Bill of Rights. Accordingly, the religious rights which the Rastafari have under section 15(1) of the Constitution are strongly reinforced by their associational rights under section 31.

In the *Pillay* case the majority and minority judgments are consistent with a modern liberal constitution even though the minority judgment is more sensitive to the religious community. To deny that groups have rights however is really to deny the communal context that facilitates the formation of culture. As Iain Benson notes in his reflection on the *Pillay* case:

> A tension always exists between understanding religion in its personal dimensions and broader communal dimensions. Too great a focus on an individual's belief runs the risk of trivialising the communal foundation to which any individual belief is invariably related. It is not too strong a statement to say that *Pillay* gets things back to front.... [T]he religious community creates and nurtures the religious believer. Unfortunately *Pillay* fails to recognise this relationship. (Benson 2008: 302; see also Lenta 2008.)

This comment turns its attention to instances of appropriate recognition of communal religious norms within the framework of the FC. I shall use two examples. The first is the recognition of customary and Islamic marriages while the second is the deference shown to determinations of the sacred and spiritual leadership of religious communities. With respect to marriage, the challenge that faces the South African legal system is its reaction to the 'other' marriages that contemplate multiple spouses and were thus different from the dominant single spouse paradigm. The Recognition Act is legislation pursuant to section 15(3) of the FC[14] and a fitting response to the challenge of the 'other' marriages. Describing the Act, Moseneke DCJ said in the *Gumede* case:

> Without doubt the chief purpose of the legislation is to reform customary law in several important ways...Most importantly it seeks to jettison gendered inequality within marriage and the marital power of the husband by providing for the equal status and capacity of spouses. ([2008] ZACC 23, para. 24. See also Herbst and du Plessis 2008.)

Since it is not true that customary law is built entirely on patriarchy it is therefore possible that by separating status from content customary law can still be

[14] Above, note 11.

legitimate. For example recognising the equal worth of women protects them in many aspects of marriage as the Recognition Act has done and still recognizes alternative forms of marriage including customary marriages. Adequate sensitivity to the reality of Muslim marriages has also been achieved through the relatively recent judicial recognition of some instances of (Muslim) Islamic marriages.[15] In *Daniels v Campbell NO and Others* ([2004] ZACC 14; 2004 5 SA 331(CC)) the CC held that the word 'spouse' in section 1 f of the Intestate Succession Act 1987 included the husband or wife in a monogamous Muslim marriage. In *Hassan v Jacobs NO* ([2009] ZACC 19) the CC included the spouses of polygynous Muslim marriages in this definition. It is clear that by recognizing spouses married under Muslim law, it deferred to norms of that law in deciding who was or was not a spouse. If it were a fact that the women in *Daniels* and *Hassan* were not regarded as married under Muslim Law, there would have been no question of considering them as spouses.

The second example is the deference shown to the decisions of spiritual and sacred leadership taken to protect their community. A number of cases reveal the willingness of the South African judiciary to protect communal religious rights in this respect. In *Taylor v Kurstag NO* (2004 4 All SA 317(W)) the Court upheld an edict of a Jewish Ecclesiastical Court effectively excommunicating a member from the Jewish society for failing to comply with its decision. The applicant argued that the excommunication breached his right to freedom of religion and freedom of association. The Court denied the application and held that the edict was a reasonable and justifiable limitation on the rights of the applicant and that rights of the community superseded the rights of the applicant because a failure to enforce the ruling of the Jewish Court would result in inability of the Jewish faith to protect the integrity of Jewish law. In *Johan Strydom v Nederduitse Gereformeerde Gemeente Moreleta Park* (2009 4 SA 510(T), [2008] ZAGPHC 269) the Equality Court was prepared to accept that religious bodies were likely to be exempted from compliance with legislation prohibiting unfair discrimination. The complainant in this case had instituted proceedings in terms of the Promotion of Equality and Prevention of Unfair Discrimination Act alleging unfair discrimination on the basis of sexual orientation.

---

[15] The legislative recognition of Islamic marriages is still pending. A bill – the Muslim Marriages Bill - proposed by the South African Law Reform Commission has not yet appeared.

It appears from a review of the manner in which religious communities are protected that the CC has exhibited a less than wholehearted willingness to protect group rights. While it is plausible claim that there was a perceptible shift in the *Pillay* case towards a more rounded understanding of the community the fact remains that the group rights of religious communities have been at the mercy of an individual rights reading. It is possible to imagine therefore that the *Shilubana* case heralds a new era where the CC will show a better appreciation of communities and of their norms. This reading is also buttressed by the evidence of lower courts showing appropriate deference to the internal norms of religious communities.

Concluding Remarks: A Unified Interpretation of 'Community' and a Beneficial Recognition of Group Rights

A plausible conclusion from a review of sections III and IV is that there is an inadequate recognition of group rights even within the options permissible under the liberal ethos of the FC. If there is no reason why other racial communities cannot have their customary law, this may enable a neutral reading of 'customary law' as entitling all racial communities to the recognition of their customary law within the constitutional framework. From this perspective it can be argued that, if the intent of the constitutional recognition of customary law is not to provide better protection for the 'black' community relative to other racial communities, all communities can seek protection either by virtue of customary law or by the protection offered by sections 30 and 31 of the FC. This comment contends that the deference shown in the *Shilubana* case heralds an appropriate model for the treatment of communal norms and that, even though the case is concerned with a black community, it is also fitting as a model for protection offered by sections 30 and 31 of the FC. What is important is the notion of communities and a desire to promote the norms within the constitutional framework. It ought to be pointed out that this view does not seek to homogenize the communities and treat all of them in the same way. Already FC 31 speaks of 'cultural, religious and linguistic communities' and it is obviously implicit in the understanding of communities that they are different. Each community comes with its own characteristics and these must be clarified before a consideration of the nature of claims it makes or which are made on its behalf.

I dare to suggest that the differentiated meaning of communities in FC 31 appears better than the hotchpotch that is customary law. It is a fact that customary law differs from place to place and that there is no 'black' community but many 'black communities'.[16] It is due to the homogenizing processes of the common law courts through the use of judicial precedent and judicial notice that there appears to be one (black) customary law in South Africa. If the defining feature of customary law is the usages and practices adopted by a people, it appears that, while many customs and usages may be similar, there will be significant differences that differentiate even the smaller members of major racial groups. Furthermore customary law does not properly represent the distinctive socially constructed groups within a society. For example religion as a common factor may be lost within the rubric of customary law, as is the case of traditional African religions (Amaoh Bennett 2008; Mutua 1999). At first blush it may be thought that black communities might be better off with the constitutional protection of customary law when it seems easier to protect them in terms of sections 30 and 31 of the FC.

The protection of cultural communities contemplates emergent communities beyond those organized around the traditional factors of language, ancestry and religion. A good example is the people including South Africans from diverse ethnic and language backgrounds that live in urban areas (see Foblets and Reyntjens 1998) and socialize because of geographical contiguity and therefore develop common interests which may include the fear of violence. This will include the gated communities in South Africa that may qualify as cultural communities deserving of the protection of the FC section 31. The notion of a community perhaps forces an inquiry into the nature of the community in contention and examines how their claim to normative recognition is reconciled with the letter, spirit and values of the FC.

A non-racial understanding of customary law is important for a more beneficial understanding of 'communities' in South Africa. Associating customary law with the black community assumes that the black community is substantially and qualitatively different from other communities in South Africa. This difference is

[16] FC s. 6(1) recognizes at least nine 'black' languages - Sepedi, Sesotho, Setswana, siSwati, Tshivenda, Xitsonga, IsiNdebele, IsiXhosa and isiZulu as official languages. It also recognizes English and Afrikaans as official languages. FC s. 6(5) establishes a Pan South African language Board to promote and create conditions for the development and use of the official languages, the Khoi, Nama and San languages as well as to promote and ensure respect for all languages used by communities in South Africa including German, Greek, Gujarat, Hindi, Portugese, Tamil, Tetegu, and Urdu.

pejorative and degrading since it is conceived in a traditional pre-modern manner. South African blacks are different from other communities just as other communities are different from them. However all these communities live in a post-modern state and there does not appear to be any reason why they ought to be treated differently in a post-apartheid state. An equal treatment of communities according to their distinct characteristics is consistent with a non-racial nation which is the objective of the FC. The FC does not deny the racial identity of South Africans by declaring that South Africa shall be a non racial nation. Rather what is prohibited is a society in which biological ancestry is the fundamental ordering. When FC section 3(1) speaks of a common South African citizenship, it contemplates plural identities/loyalties. Amongst these identities are first, a national identity which is built on an equal entitlement as human beings to the rights, privileges, benefits and duties of citizenship (Mamdani 1998). Another identity can be formed by communities socially constructed on differentiating factors such as race, language and religion which brand communities that nurture, encourage and sustain self-worth and respect. It is these communities that the *Shilubana* case invites us to recognize, promote, respect and protect.

References

AMOAH, Jewel and Tom BENNETT

2008 'The freedoms of religion and culture under the South African Constitution: Do traditional African religions enjoy equal treatment?' *African Human Rights Law Journal* 8: 357-375.

BENNETT, Tom

2005 *Human Rights and African Customary Law* Cape Town Juta.

2009 'Re-introducing African customary law to the South African legal system' *American Journal of Comparative Law* 57: 1-31.

BENSON, Iain

2008 'The case for religious inclusivism and the judicial recognition of religious associational rights: a response to Lenta.' *Constitutional Court Review* 1: 295-310.

BRAY, Eva

2007 'Macro issues of Mikro Primary School' 10 : 1-20.

FLEISCH, Brahm and Stuart WOOLMAN

2007 'On the constitutionality of single-medium public schools.' *South African Journal on Human Rights* 23: 34-67.

FOBLETS, Marie-Claire and Filip REYNTJENS (eds.)
1998 *Urban Normative Fields in Africa Today/ Champs Normatifs Urbains en Afrique Contemporaine. Special Issue Journal of Legal Pluralism* 42.

HIMONGA, Chuma and Craig BOSCH
2000 'The application of African customary law under the Constitution of South Africa: Problems solved or just beginning?' *South African Law Journal* 117: 306-341.

KAGANAS, Felicity and Christina MURRAY
1994 The contest between culture and gender equality under South Africa's Interim Constitution' *Journal of Law and Society* 21:409-433.

LEHNERT, Wieland
2005 'The role of the courts in the conflict between African customary law and human rights' *South African Journal on Human Rights* 21: 241-277.

LENTA, Patrick
2008 'Cultural and religious accommodations to school uniform regulations.' *Constitutional Court Review* 1: 259.

LEVY, Jacob T.
1997 'Classifying cultural rights.' Pp. 22-66 in Will Kymlicka and Ian Shapiro (eds.), *Ethnicity and Group Rights* New York: New York University Press.

MAMDANI, Mahmood
1998 'When does a settler become a native? Reflections of the colonial roots of citizenship in Equatorial and South Africa' Text of Inaugural lecture 13 May 1998. Available at www.bard.edu/resource pdfs/mamdani.setller.pdf (last accessed 13 Oct 2009).

MMUSINYANE Boitumelo
2009 'The role of traditional authorities in developing customary laws in accordance with the constitution: *Shilubana and others v Nwamitwa* 2008 9 BCLR 914 (CC).' *Potchefstroom Electronic Review* 12: 136-161.

MURRAY, Christina and Richard SIMEON
2007 'Recognition without empowerment: Minorities in a democratic South Africa.' *International Journal of Constitutional Law* 5 699-729.

MUTUA, Makua wa
1999 'Limitations on religious rights: Problematising religious freedom in the African context.' *Buffalo Human Rights Review* 5: 75-105.

OOMEN, Barbara
1999 'Group rights in post-apartheid South Africa: The case of the traditional leaders.' *Journal of Legal Pluralism* 44: 73-103.

PIETERSE, Marius
2001 'It's a "Black Thing": Upholding culture and customary law in a society founded on non-racialism.' *South African Journal on Human Rights* 17: 364-403.

RAUTENBACH, Christa
2003 'Some comments on the status of customary law in relation to the Bill of Rights.' *Stellenbosch Law Review* 14: 107-114.

THE POLITICS OF LEGAL PLURALISM: STATE POLICIES ON LEGAL PLURALISM AND THEIR LOCAL DYNAMICS IN MOZAMBIQUE[1]

Helene Maria Kyed

Introduction

What happens when legal pluralism becomes a policy concept? Or put differently: what are the consequences when legal pluralism enters national laws and policies and thereby ceases to be solely an analytical concept used by scholars to address the plurality of normative orders and institutions that enforce order within a political organisation? The exact meaning of the concept of legal pluralism is still debated, and not all agree on its normative value, with some arguing for the superiority of state law and others for the equality of legal orders.[2] Despite this, legal pluralism is today increasingly accepted as an empirical 'fact' not only by a

[1] An earlier draft version of this article was presented at the international workshop, *Customary Justice and Legal Pluralism in Post-Conflict and Fragile Societies*, George Washington University, November 17-18, 2009.

[2] Legal pluralism as an analytical concept has been debated extensively by socio-legal scholars, and it is not the purpose of this article to rehash this debate here (see Griffiths 1986; Tamanaha 2000, 2008; Woodman 1998; Benda-Beckmann et al. 2009). This article is confined to a discussion of the implications of legal pluralism as a 'policy concept', which to my knowledge has been much less addressed.

wide range of socio-legal disciplines, but also by some governments in the South and by international organisations engaged with justice and security issues in developing countries. State law and its institutions, it is acknowledged, do not have monopoly on ordering society, but co-exist with other institutions and normative orders, whether referred to as 'informal', 'customary', 'religious', or 'non-state'.

Legal pluralism as a *policy concept* is reflected in state laws and constitutions that recognise legal pluralism as a principle describing the justice system of the country.[3] It is also present in many current development donor programs and strategies that now focus on the significance of non-state justice and security providers (OECD/DAC 2007; World Bank 2008; Danida 2009; UNDP/Wojkowska 2006; DFID 2004). This marks a shift from their earlier exclusive focus on support for state-legal institutions. International human rights documents also increasingly embrace legal pluralism, and a number of NGOs, national and international, are now engaging with non-state actors who solve conflicts and provide justice.[4]

As a policy concept, legal pluralism tends in official discourse to convey recognition of the socio-cultural diversity of the legal domain within a nation state. This is exemplified by the import of non-state 'law' into state law and by the recognition of the role in providing justice or handling disputes, of existing non-state authorities such as traditional leaders or chiefs, clan elders, and religious institutions.[5] It may also take the form of state or international support for the establishment of new hybrid, community-based mediation and conflict resolution mechanisms that draw on local norms and procedures while also being informed by state and international legal standards such as human rights. Inclusion and recognition of non-state legal orders and justice mechanisms differs from the

[3] Legal pluralism as a policy principle describing the entire justice system of a nation-state differs from a situation in which the state recognises selected non-state, customary or informal justice providers or 'laws', which has occurred for a long time, including during colonial rule (see Mommsen and de Moor 1991).

[4] On the recognition of legal pluralism in Human Rights Declarations, General Comments and Covenants, especially those relating to indigenous people and minorities, see ICHRP (2009: 27-31).

[5] On a discussion of the term non-state law, and to what extent the term 'law' can be used to refer to non-state normative orders (see Woodman 1998; Tamanaha 2008; Moore 1978).

previous dominance of state-legal centralism in national frameworks and in international support for justice and security sector reform.[6]

This article explores the consequences of legal pluralism as a 'policy concept', using the example of post-war Mozambique, where legal pluralism has gained constitutional recognition since 2004. It engages in a discussion of what I term 'the politics of legal pluralism'. This 'politics' denotes the, often covert, political interests behind legal pluralism policies and the political implications of how such policies are put into effect. Despite official discourse, I argue, legal pluralism as a 'policy field' seldom implies only a simple or benign recognition of the empirical manifestations of socio-cultural diversity. It also implies a framework for state intervention, regulation and reform, and so has political implications.

Drawing on extensive fieldwork in rural and urban Mozambique, I argue for the need to critically scrutinize the official policy claims that underpin legal pluralism, and which tend to mask key political aspects. Such claims often posit legal pluralism as reflecting the peaceful coexistence of distinct normative orders or legal 'systems'. The recognition by the state of such plurality is presented in official discourse as an unproblematic, apolitical embracing of socio-cultural diversity and even as a win-win situation for state and non-state 'legal systems'. This overlooks a reality of competing, partly overlapping jurisdictions and diverse claims to authority.[7] As a result of this reality, legal pluralism often becomes not a pure recognition of 'what already exists' empirically, but a means by which the state attempts to establish what policy claims posit: distinct 'legal systems'. This translates into state efforts to regulate non-state justice providers, (re)define their areas of jurisdiction, and establish a hierarchical boundary between 'legal systems'.[8] Central to such boundary-making are efforts to assert the superior

[6] The concept of state-legal centralism refers to the ideologically informed claim that "[...] law is and should be the law of the state, uniform for all persons, exclusive of all other law, and administered by a single set of state institutions" (Griffiths 1986: 3).

[7] On the need to view legal pluralism as describing a situation of various layers of merger and intermix of justice systems, see for example Santos (2006), who usefully introduces the concept of inter-legality to describe such a situation. Inter-legality has come about as the result of long histories of interaction in which justice systems have evolved together. On a similar point, see Tamanaha (2008).

[8] I place quotation marks around the concept of 'legal systems', because, while

authority of the state, its laws and institutions.

State recognition of non-state legal orders is therefore not a technical, neutral process, but an inherently political one. The state legitimises the authority of non-state justice providers, but also assumes the authority to define what counts as legitimate non-state justice institutions and rules. The result is restrictions on how non-state justice providers can operate, which has implications for how they assert authority. Thus while recognition of legal pluralism can be an instance of state law adapting to local socio-cultural norms, it also involves a re-ordering of authority and power. Recognition can also be appropriated to boost the popular legitimacy of state institutions or to avoid conflicts in contested, post-war contexts, through alliances with non-state authorities. It can also become an instrument of the political party in power to consolidate its local power base and to mobilise votes in the context of transitions to multiparty democracy. Similar political objectives may where legal pluralism policies involve the establishment of 'new' hybrid institutions defined as 'community-based', 'informal' or 'non-state', such as in the case of community policing councils and community courts in Mozambique. The difference is that here we are not speaking about state recognition of already existing non-state legal orders, but of an institutional expansion of the non-state domain in the name of accommodating local 'community' norms or customs.

The *politics of legal pluralism* is not, however, the exclusive purview of state officials and party politicians. Non-state providers can also use state recognition as a source of authority to enforce decisions or to assert power vis-à-vis other non-state authorities. In fact, local state efforts to apply legal pluralism policy may further invigorate competition between state and non-state providers over authority and 'clients'.

The core argument of this article is therefore that legal pluralism as a policy concept easily becomes the subject of political manipulation or itself is a political

official discourse and policies on legal pluralism tend to speak of 'systems', this claim does not necessarily correspond to the empirical reality of often more loosely structured mechanisms of justice, overlapping jurisdictions and clusters of rules or institutions. The term 'system' rather denotes structured and relatively comprehensive bodies of law (see Woodman 1998). Or as held by Griffiths, who prefers the term 'legal order', a 'system' has "overtones of completeness, orderliness, institutionalization, and static equilibrium" (Griffiths 1986: 12).

tool to assert authority and manifest power. This, I argue, is intimately related to the politics of justice provision itself, and by extension of social ordering: providing justice or policing order is a key source of authority, and often an avenue to income and resources.

As I illustrate with the Mozambican case, the politics of legal pluralism can cover at least three layers of politics. The first is the politics of asserting the superior authority of state institutions and law over other legal orders. This is exemplified by the use of legal pluralism by the state to regulate non-state providers and redefine their areas of jurisdiction. It can also take the form of the state outsourcing functions to non-state actors, but in a way that supports state authority. The second layer is the political party interests in non-state justice and security providers, which can emerge as a result of transitions to multiparty democracy. This is exemplified by the use of legal pluralism to boost the power of politicians or the regime in power by ways of creating alliances with non-state authorities or by using them to hit at the political opposition. Finally, the politics of legal pluralism is also expressed in local-level contestations over power and 'clients' to sustain the authority of a given institution or personal power positions, including those of local state officials, such as the police. This aspect often predates legal pluralism policies, and may even be one of its causes, but can be exacerbated by or take new forms as a result of legal pluralism policies.

In the remainder of this article I address first the national politics behind the state recognition of legal pluralism in Mozambique. I then explore the politics of legal pluralism in practice in a rural district, particularly focusing on the state recognition of traditional authority since 2002. Thirdly, I examine community policing in an urban setting, and show how, as a new model of non-state involvement in security provision, it is politically instrumentalized by the state police and the ruling party. Finally, I conclude with some reflections on what I consider important political aspects to be considered in international support for and studies of legal pluralism policies.

The Politics behind State Recognition of Legal Pluralism

In Mozambique legal pluralism was officially recognised in the 2004 revised Constitution:

> the state recognises the various normative and dispute resolution

> systems that co-exist in Mozambican society, insofar as they are not contrary to the fundamental principles and values of the Constitution (Republic of Mozambique 2004: art. 4).

The Constitution also calls for institutional and procedural mechanisms that link formal-state courts with other, non-state mechanisms of justice (ibid.: art. 212). This official commitment to legal pluralism is reiterated in the Government's Integrated Strategic Plan for the Justice Sector (PEI II, 2008-2012), which should be the framework for any government initiatives and donor-supported programs on the justice sector. This marks a clear shift in policy.

The constitutional recognition of legal pluralism can be seen as the cumulative effect of an increased shift from state legal centralism towards state recognition of non-state, community-based and customary authorities since the 16-year civil war ended in 1992 and the country embarked on a democratic transition. Until 2000 donor support to justice sector reform focused exclusively on reforming formal state institutions in accordance with 'the rule of law' and 'human rights'. The village-level popular courts established by the socialist regime in the 1980s, and comprising lay judges using procedures based on local customs, were delinked from the formal court system, renamed 'community courts' and downgraded to informal conflict resolution bodies. Village secretaries and popular vigilantes, who formed part of the Frelimo-state structures to resolve conflicts and maintain order at the local level, were also excluded in post-war legislation. Reform of the justice sector further ignored those non-state justice providers such as chiefs, traditional healers and religious leaders who, outside state law, played a significant role in justice enforcement on the ground (Kyed 2009a).[9] Overall justice sector reform focused on not only democratising the formal system and making it more effective, but also on re-extending state institutions and law to the vast territories of the country where these had been weakened or had disappeared because of the protracted war. Non-state institutions were seen as an impediment to this development. Implicitly it was assumed that they would no longer be significant once the state legal system was in place.

---

[9] After independence in 1975, chiefs and traditional healers were officially banned by the Frelimo government. With regard to chiefs, this marked a clear break from colonial indirect rule, which had relied on chiefs. However, in practice many chiefs continued to perform significant roles in justice enforcement and policing. Some also supported the rebel movement Renamo during the war (Kyed 2007a).

The drive towards recognition of legal pluralism in 2004 resulted partly from changes in donor trends and partly from the meagre results of initial reform efforts. Formal state institutions were still not able to provide adequate justice and security, were corrupt and lacked popular legitimacy. This was confirmed by a number of studies in the 1990s, which provided evidence of the continued significance of traditional authority and other forms of non-state justice providers. One particularly influential donor-funded study argued that the formal system ignored the needs of the poor, who preferred restorative to punitive justice (Trindade and Santos 2003). It held that the judicial system ought to be adjusted to this reality through legal and functional linkages between the formal courts, community justice and traditional authorities, thus establishing a *de jure* system of legal pluralism. This would make the justice system more efficient and better adjusted to local socio-cultural notions of justice (Trindade and Santos 2003: 581-582).

There were also clear political interests behind the recognition of legal pluralism. Studies arguing for the role of traditional authority in administration, conflict resolution and national identity formation instigated intensive media and parliamentary debates between the ruling party, Frelimo and the opposition, Renamo. While Frelimo was split on the issue, Renamo wanted full recognition of traditional authority. However, after the 1999 elections, the Frelimo government became convinced that Renamo had a strong voter-base in many rural areas because it had aligned itself with chiefs during the war. On the ground this was matched by conflicts between traditional authorities and former Frelimo village secretaries, as well as by pockets of resistance by chiefs to the state police and administrators. Simultaneously, local state officials began to depend on informal collaboration with traditional authorities to re-establish state institutional outreach in the rural areas. The Frelimo party structures also benefited from such alliances (see Kyed 2007a).

Thus in 2000 the Frelimo government passed a ministerial decree, Decree 15/2000, which conceded recognition of both traditional authorities and the (former Frelimo) village secretaries as 'community authorities'.[10] Aside from a range of state administrative tasks, these authorities were obligated to assist the

[10] It is important to note that the recognition of traditional authority is based on a decree and not a law, which means that it was approved not by Parliament, but by the Council of Ministers. This reflects, I suggest, the Frelimo government's desire to decide itself the terms of this recognition.

police and courts in order enforcement and conflict resolution. In return they received uniforms and subsidies from the state. The Frelimo government also committed itself to strengthening the role of the community courts, by measures which included improving the election procedures and establishing links to the formal courts.[11] However, this was a less politically controversial area for the government, because existing community court judges were already associated with the ruling party, these courts having been substituted for the former popular courts. The recognition of village secretaries under the same title as traditional authorities was also seen by Renamo as a means to ensure that some 'community authorities' came from Frelimo ranks.

These political interests lying behind state recognition of non-state institutions, and merging party politics with the extension of state administrative powers, have, unsurprisingly, been masked in the official policy claims that have underpinned the subsequent constitutional recognition of legal pluralism. Officially legal pluralism policies have been cast as state recognition of 'what already exists', namely traditional and community-based forms of justice that draw on the socio-cultural norms of the variety of local communities across the country. The 1992 law on community courts and Decree 15/2000 also posit the unproblematic co-existence of state and non-state institutions, as representing distinct domains of justice enforcement which handle different issues and which can mutually benefit from collaboration. In short, non-state institutions have been portrayed as institutions that do not compete with the state police and courts in the types of problems they solve or in their claims to authority.

While this policy claim has little resonance in practice, as I argue below, it may help to explain why the recognition of legal pluralism has not been supported by any clear legal framework outlining the respective roles, mandates and jurisdictions of the patchwork of non-state institutions that co-exist within the same geographical areas (i.e. community courts, traditional leaders, village secretaries, traditional healers). Nor has any substantial legislation specified how these

[11] In 1998 associations of traditional healers were also officially recognized. However, since official law denies the existence of sorcery, recognition of the authority and scope of action of healers only extends to traditional medical treatment of illnesses, and not to any role of healers in conflict resolution (West 2005).

institutions should interact with the formal justice system, despite the clear constitutional requirement. Whereas the 2005 draft legislation on judicial reform envisioned an integrated judicial system with legal and functional interaction between the formal courts and non-state justice providers, the actual legislation passed in 2007, the Organic Law of the Judicial Courts (Law 24/2007), merely notes that judicial courts "may articulate with other existing conflict resolution instances" (Republic of Mozambique 2007: art. 6). There is no mention of what 'instances' this may include or how such articulation may be put into effect. The law does introduce the possibility of an appeal system between community courts and district courts, but it is unclear exactly how this should work (ibid.: art. 5). Thus, what exists is a set of dispersed laws and decrees that recognize different non-state authorities' role in conflict resolution.

This patchwork of non-state actors, recognised by the state, has more recently been expanded with the introduction of community policing councils (CPCs), the agents of which also engage in conflict resolution and, unofficially, act as judges (Kyed 2009b). While a decree on this area is not expected to be approved by the Council of Ministers until some time during 2010, CPCs have been implemented by the Ministry of Interior (MINT) since 2001 in a few selected urban areas, with initial support from the German bilateral donor GTZ, and since 2005 in the whole country. The CPCs are intended to be comprised of influential local citizens, who are elected by the local community. They are meant to discuss and gather information on local security problems and perform patrols with the state police. As envisioned by MINT, CPCs are expected to mediate conflicts, such as those involving land disputes, disagreements between neighbours and family disputes. However, they are not allowed to handle crimes, which are supposed to remain the exclusive purview of the state police (MINT 2005). So envisioned, the roles of CPCs overlap in significant ways with already existing non-state authorities, such as chiefs and community courts, but there are no formally established linkages between them.

Drawing first on the case of the rural district of Sussundenga, I tentatively suggest that what appears to be a reluctance to pass a law or develop a strategy on institutional linkages and mandates arises not only from questions of policy claims about non-state legal orders and their relationship to the state. It is also informed by the politics behind legal pluralism. Lack of clear mandates and of legal mechanisms for monitoring non-state institutions leaves ample room for political instrumentalization by local state officials and ruling party cadres. In fact, as I argue next, the stifled policy-making process at national level has been overtaken by developments on the ground.

Rural Politics of Legal Pluralism – the Case of Community Authorities

Despite the absence of a clear legal framework, official recognition of legal pluralism has in practice been appropriated by local state officials as a *de facto* 'framework for action' in the rural areas. It has been used not only to endorse, but also to regulate non-state justice providers and to (re)define their respective jurisdictions vis-à-vis the state. The result is that different kinds of articulation in essence take place *outside of* official law. While the framework for action brings somewhat more clarity to the plural legal landscape and aims to provide more effective case-handling, it is driven by local state and party political interests.

At least in some areas, the *de facto* framework for legal pluralism has been used to (re)expand the outreach of the state in areas where state authority is contested or weak. In such instances local state articulation with non-state institutions is often aimed at subjugating those who have competing sovereign claims, i.e. who, like the state, claim the ultimate authority to define and prosecute severe transgressions. This process has merged with efforts to re-vitalize or strengthen those non-state institutions that are loyal to the ruling party, Frelimo, such as the community courts and the village secretaries, and to create alliances with those who historically have not been, such as traditional healers and chiefs. Such efforts are, however, contested in everyday case-handling, and coexist with competition, as different actors defend their jurisdiction in order to protect power interests and to maintain their authority.

The initial ground for local state appropriation of legal pluralism was laid during the process of state recognition of traditional leaders or chiefs, which began in 2001-2. A good example of this process can be seen in the rural district of Sussundenga in Manica Province. [12]

[12] The example of Sussundenga District is based on extensive fieldwork in 2002, 2004 and 2005, and updated field-visits in 2007 and 2009. For a more detailed discussion of the process of state recognition of chiefs, see Kyed and Buur 2006; Kyed 2007a.

Asserting state authority and ruling party power

Sussundenga district was a hotly contested area during the civil war. The rural areas outside the administrative capital were controlled by Renamo, and some chiefs, from the mid-1980s. The state institutions, including the police, popular courts and village secretaries, were essentially dissolved. Renamo's influence in this area continued to be strong after the end of the civil war. In the mid-1990s there were pockets of open resistance by Renamo and some chiefs towards state police and the administrative (re)establishment outside the district capital.

Decree 15/2000, allowing for the state recognition of chiefs, became an essential tool to reverse the situation of state weakness in Sussundenga. It gave local state officials a tool to establish alliances with chiefs in the contested territories, based on promises not only of official recognition, but also of development benefits and state subsidies. Such promises initially sparked conflicts among different candidates to chieftaincies, as war, migration and shifting alliances had considerably reshuffled traditional authority positions and territorial jurisdictions. While state officials accepted 'traditional' criteria of leadership selection, there were instances in which state officials intervened to support candidates that showed loyalty to the state and the ruling party.[13]

The alliances that recognition enabled became direct means of the territorial-institutional expansion of the state. In the most rural hinterlands recognition was followed by the re-establishment of police posts, administrative offices and Frelimo party cells. In one area, the recognition ceremony for a chief also marked the first visit of a post-colonial state administrator to the area. Such encounters allowed state administrators, always accompanied by police officers and Frelimo secretaries, to engage with and promulgate the government's program to the rural population. Later recognition has also facilitated everyday forms of state governance, as chiefs are obligated to collect personal tax, produce population registers, and denounce criminals to the police. While local state officials place emphasis on the value of the 'traditions' of which chiefs are custodians, the general message is that state recognition means that chiefs 'now have to obey the orders of the government'.[14] This has merged with party political requirements.

[13] On this process of selection, see Kyed 2007a; Buur and Kyed 2006.

[14] For a discussion of tradition not as a fixed, but a mutable set of rules and practices, see West and Kloeck-Jenson 1999; Buur and Kyed 2007; Moore 1986; Oomen 2005; Handler and Linnekin 1984.

Chiefs are drawn into election campaigns, sometimes being obliged to mobilize votes for Frelimo and display its posters at their homesteads. Chiefs are also expected to hold Frelimo membership cards in order to draw their benefits from the state. While some chiefs still covertly support Renamo, and many of them stage compliance only at public state meetings, the message is that their state-recognized authority is conditional on their politics, i.e. loyalty to Frelimo.

From 2003 the local politics of legal pluralism were expanded with the revitalization of village secretaries and the establishment of community courts at the sub-district level. In contrast to legal requirements for community election, village secretaries and community court judges were appointed by a group consisting of the First Frelimo secretary, the local administrator, and the chief of the police. The history of the candidates shows that they had all had roles in the former Frelimo-state structures, with many having been in exile in the Frelimo-controlled areas during the war. Thus, while a criterion for appointment was knowledge of conflict resolution and local customs, the choice of Frelimo-loyal adjudicators can also be seen as part of the effort to consolidate party-state power.

The year 2004 also saw an increased effort by the state police, which still continues, in coordination with administrators, to regulate what in essence had become a rather complex and competitive field of justice enforcement and policing. These developments have continued since that year. The reason for this is that community courts and village secretaries claim jurisdictions that in effect overlap with chiefs' courts. They settle some of the same types of cases, apply similar justice procedures and outcomes, issue client fees and have a fixed weekly day for court sessions. More importantly, the chiefs also claim forms of authority that overlap with the criminal law jurisdiction of the state. This includes the right to settle severe crimes and enforce non-negotiable penalties akin to those prescribed by statutory law. For chiefs this covers homicide as in state courts, but also violation of sacred places and disrespect for authority. At times chiefs' courts also resort to physical punishment, which challenges the state's claim to a monopoly on the use of legitimate force.

At sub-district level the local state police, who alone represent the formal justice system at the sub-district level, have played a vital role in trying to bring some semblance of order to this field of overlapping jurisdictions. This they have done by enforcing what in effect is a new form of *local police law* comprising *de facto* rules for articulation and jurisdiction. It is enforced in the name of 'state law', but clearly differs from it. In some ways the local police law even violates codified law by allowing for the arbitration of sorcery and endorsing extra-legal sanctions against non-compliant chiefs and other non-state arbitrators.

The *local police law* recognizes three general categories of cases, namely, social, traditional and criminal, which serve as the basis for assigning jurisdiction. Non-state providers are strictly prohibited from handling any serious crimes, i.e. acts that violate the land and inflict violence on human bodies: homicides, fights in which blood is spilt, rapes, large thefts, armed robberies and arson. Community courts and village secretaries are only allowed to handle what the police refer to as 'social cases', such as adultery, physical assaults without bleeding, minor threats and insults, divorce cases, marriage payment disputes and land disputes between neighbours. Finally, so-called 'traditional cases' are reserved for chiefs. The local police law recognizes sorcery as a traditional case and requires that such cases are referred to chiefs. However, because the police prohibit chiefs from handling serious crimes, the police definition of 'traditional cases' excludes a whole series of offences – such as the taking of life – that chiefs, and many other local citizens, consider to have a 'traditional dimension'. As a result traditional rules are redefined by the police.

The local police law also sets out procedures for case-handling in social and traditional cases among the non-state institutions, including a prohibition on the use of expulsion and physical force. The police also require chiefs to arrest and report criminal suspects, and bring them to the police post. This in effect turns chiefs into an extension of the police, although it is still an offence if chiefs resolve crimes, or if they use force. The police do not hesitate to resort to extra-legal sanctions to enforce 'their' law. On several occasions chiefs have been punished with physical force, or through mandatory public work and/or days of incarceration for disobeying local police law. While recognizing local justice mechanisms and using chiefs to boost their enforcing power in the hinterlands, the police have thus criminalized significant justice enforcement practices of chiefs that underwrite their authority within local communities. Ultimately, even if enforced by formal law officials, this system of local police law operates largely apart from the formal court system.[15]

In the final analysis, the practice and structure of the local police law is driven by

[15] 2004-5 formal court case settlement figures for Sussundenga shows that only 13% of the criminal cases and 3% of the civil cases were handled by the formal courts.

a variety of overlapping power interests. Foremost among these is the local police interest in consolidating the state's monopoly on the handling of crimes, the allocation of litigation, and the use of force. However, in practice, the personal power interests of local police officers and their interest in defending their authority vis-à-vis non-state authorities often merges with and is rather difficult to distinguish from broader interests in protecting state sovereignty. Partisan political power is also often at stake, and is an interest that plays an accentuated role in how local law plays out in practice. This is exemplified by random arrests of and excessive punishments of Renamo supporters (see more in Kyed 2007b). However, as I shall show next, the 'law' of the local police has not been without challenges in everyday case-handling.

The politics of local contestations over authority

The 'law' of the local police is frequently contested, even by state police officers themselves. Despite collaboration with the police, chiefs continue to settle crimes, some of them serious: in 2004-5 they resolved 21% of the crimes in Sussundenga.[16] Many community courts and village secretaries also fail to comply with the requirement to forward 'traditional cases' such as sorcery to chiefs. People frequently take their cases to the 'wrong' authorities or 'forum shop' between them. Interviews with citizens suggest that this occurs not because people are unaware of the local police law but because it can be a strategic means to gain desired outcomes (Kyed 2007a). It also has to do with a discrepancy between police categories of cases and local views of what constitutes justice. As a result the local police law has had a number of unintended consequences.

In Sussundenga it is common that a case of crime, such as theft, results in witchcraft accusations or that a crime, such as arson or homicide, is seen as also having an evil spiritual dimension. Rural citizens prefer to have such disputes resolved holistically as they have been in chiefs' courts. Settling crimes with chiefs or other non-state providers is also preferred because of the emphasis on compensation for the victim. By contrast, formal court resolutions are associated with imprisonment, which most rural citizens view as payment to the state, not to the victims. Thus victims themselves often beg chiefs to refrain from forwarding crimes to the police. For chiefs the continued practice of settling crimes can

[16] Figures are based on fieldwork conducted in Sussundenga District (see Kyed 2007a).

therefore be seen as a response to popular demands. At the same time it brings in important client fees. Much the same can be said for the handling of sorcery cases by village secretaries and community courts. Conversely, most chiefs also began in 2004, as a result of engagement with the state police, to make oral reference to state law and to highlight their status as state-recognized authorities when they, in opposition to the police's law, handled criminal cases. For example by threatening to send parties to the police, the chiefs manage to enforce sanctions better. The community courts and village secretaries avail themselves of similar kinds of references to state law, but as opposed to chiefs they seldom settle serious crimes.

Perhaps most intriguingly, the police themselves also began to handle sorcery and other non-criminal cases. Between 2004 and 2005 this increased from 1-2 cases per day to 3-5 cases per day. In such cases, the police use procedures that resemble those of chiefs, while also adding notifications with official stamps and threats of physical discipline to dissuade non-compliance. People thus increasingly take non-criminal cases to the police as a last resort when they fail to achieve resolution elsewhere. However, such recourse only makes sense because the police settle cases by applying principles that realize local notions of justice. Police officers are well aware that if they simply enforce the statutory law, and do not adjust to local requirements, they risk losing their status *vis-à-vis* chiefs.

In short, local police efforts to establish bounded jurisdictions between different 'systems' have resulted in new forms of procedural and jurisdictional overlap, without entirely replacing old practices. Ultimately, this result follows from contestations over authority by parties with different interests. The police face a dilemma: they depend on chiefs to enforce law and order, which underwrites police authority, yet they also feel threatened by the chiefs' capacity to draw upon locally legitimate mechanisms of enforcement that challenge state authority. For the chiefs, their authority is precarious, because local demands and criteria for justice are often at odds with state requirements. Chiefs must constantly balance their fear of punishment by the police and their own constituents' preferences.

For most rural citizens the plurality of available fora is a resource to negotiate strategically. However, it is usually the more resourceful and powerful people who can take most advantage of the plural terrain. Equal access to justice is compromised, and there are no real signs that a link to the formal courts will be forthcoming anytime soon (Kyed 2007b). From both rule of law and human rights perspectives, the practical forms of articulation pose serious challenges. Not only do the local police act as judges and law-makers, but the *de facto* situation also sustains a culture of extra-legal police violence that is deployed to protect their monopoly on the use of violence – in particular against chiefs. When this *politics of legal pluralism* merges with ruling party political interests and loyalty – as is often the case, not least around elections – then the legitimate, state-availed spaces for diversity and pluralism seem to become even more closed.

Much the same can be said of how community policing has evolved in an urban suburb of Maputo. However, here the role of ruling party politics in monopolising legal pluralism is even more articulated, and seems to dominate over state efforts to control the domain of legal ordering.

Urban Politics of Legal Pluralism – the Case of Community Policing

As in rural areas, many urban crimes and conflicts are handled outside the official legal system, some by local state officials. This is done despite geographic proximity to police stations and formal courts. For example, in poor urban suburbs of the capital city Maputo, a range of local actors and organisations make up the plural landscape of justice and policing providers. Aside from the local tiers of the state, these may include: community policing agents, 'community' leaders or heads of sub-units (*chefes dos quarterões*), community courts, organisations of traditional healers and different local organisations, churches and human rights NGOs that in one way or the other resolve conflicts, police the area, or provide legal aid. However, there is great variety between the poor suburbs of Maputo in terms of who provides justice and perform policing. There is also variation in the bodies to which different people within a given suburb prefer to go with their cases. In addition, there has been an increase in mob-justice and lynching of criminals by groups of local residents in poor urban areas especially since the mid-2000s (see Serra 2008).[17]

The poor urban *bairro* (suburb) under consideration in this article, which I shall

[17] This article will not engage in a thorough discussion of mob-justice, but it suffices to say that research in this area supports my own fieldwork findings, which conclude that mob-justice is largely a sign that people are not only dissatisfied with the formal justice system and the police, but that local, non-state institutions are also perceived by urban residents as inadequate in the punishment of criminals (see more in Serra 2008).

call *bairro A*, is characterized by a case-settlement system in which informal forms of interaction between different actors, state and non-state, have evolved through local negotiations rather than through integration with the formal legal system.[18] Much happens outside official law, and here too disagreements occur between the different providers over jurisdiction. However, if we consider how decisions are taken and who predominantly take up positions in the organs that provide justice and police the area, we find that in the *bairro* there is a much more solidified integration with the local Frelimo structures than in Sussundenga.[19] In this 'system', the state police have only partial leverage over everyday crime control.

When actually present in the area, police officers collaborate with what *de facto* is a 'semi-autonomous field' (Moore 1978) of community policing, which is operated by a group of young men. Although these men do at times take orders from the police, they are *de facto* under the control of local Frelimo cadres and the local state administrator, the *secretário do bairro*. This system is not unchallenged, however. A number of self-organised groups of *bairro* residents as well as individuals discredit or simply do not recognise the present organisation of community policing, and regularly take matters into their own hands. Much less frequently people bypass the local system of community policing and bring their matters directly to the nearest police station.

That the state police have only partial control over everyday policing in the *bairro*

---

[18] The insights presented here are based on fieldwork in a suburb of District 2 of Maputo city in May-December 2009. The *bairro* has a population of approximately 14,500 and lies on the frontier of the inner city and the area where the poor suburbs begin, which is reflected by a combination of apartment buildings on the frontier, associated with the inner city, and small houses and shacks, associated with poorer suburbs. The socio-economic make-up of the population is also relatively heterogeneous, ranging from extremely poor to people with medium incomes. The *bairro* is known as an area with high crime rates, which may be due to the fact that it has a large informal market, a zone with intensive drug-dealing and high unemployment among the youth.

[19] There may be different historical reasons for this difference between rural areas like Sussundenga and the Maputo *bairro A* under consideration. One apparent explanation could be that in *bairro A* the Frelimo leadership structures were never dissolved during the war and governance was not displaced by Renamo control as in Sussundenga district.

does not mean that they refrain from efforts to use legal pluralism to assert their superior authority within the field of law and order enforcement. However, in contrast to the tactics used in Sussundenga, in *bairro A* attempts to assert authority have been made by outsourcing functions to the young community policing actors rather than through efforts to domesticate existing non-state providers. Below, I first address this politics of outsourcing, and secondly consider how community policing has become an instrument of local ruling party politics.

The politics of state police authority: outsourcing to young men

In *bairro A* the state police are represented by a single sector police officer, who is usually present only 2-3 days a week, and by periodic patrols by uniformed officers, usually a few times a month. Since 2003 the state police have at least officially collaborated with the community policing council that was formed in the same year through an initiative taken by MINT, as in other urban *bairros* of the country.[20] According to MINT's policy, community policing councils are supposed to comprise "community leaders" and "other important social actors", who are elected by the population to debate crime solutions with the state police and assist its officers in patrolling the *bairro* (MINT 2005; Kyed 2009b). In practice, however, this council was short-lived in *bairro A*. Soon it was replaced by a *de facto* local police force made up of young men and a woman in her early fifties who acts as the coordinator. In late 2009 there were a total of eleven community policing agents between the ages of 22 and 33.

On a daily basis the young men perform a range of 'traditional' police functions, including *inter alia*: patrols, arrests of suspects and persons caught committing crimes or disturbing public order, control of people for IDs, search of persons in public spaces for drugs and stolen goods, investigations of thefts and recovery of stolen goods, and even hearings and resolution of cases. The eleven men are seldom all on duty at the same time, but at least two of them turn up every day to work from the *circulo* – the name for the central governance site of a *bairro*, which also houses the *secretário do bairro*, the sector police officer and the Frelimo party branch. Patrols and searches are often performed alone by the community policing agents and only at times with state police officers.

[20] Community policing was first launched in 2001 in a few pilot project areas of Maputo and Manica province. Only in 2005 was it expanded to rural areas.

Resolution of cases by the community policing agents is carried out in a room of the *circulo* that has been granted to the community police by the *secretário do bairro*. It mainly covers crimes such as thefts, particularly of cell-phones, trade in stolen goods, fraud, physical assaults, drug-dealing and consumption, and burglaries. Some cases are forwarded to the police station, usually when the sector police officer is present or when the community policing agents give up hope of solving a case themselves. In the latter case it is usually the community policing agents who accompany the accused to the police station, either alone or together with the sector police officer. However, when case records made by the community police themselves between 2007 and 2009 are compared with the monthly statistics reported by the sector police, it becomes clear that the majority of criminal cases are settled or at least brought to an end within the walls of the *circulo*.[21] The types of resolutions used by the community policing agents include compensational justice, including return of stolen goods, reconciliation of disputing parties, and corporal punishment using batons. The community policing agents also frequently use physical force as an 'investigation' technique within the walls of the *circulo*.[22] Other investigation techniques include the seeking of information from other *bairro* residents, including criminals whom the community policing agents know because they are residents of the *bairro*.

These extensive crime resolution practices of the community police starkly contradict MINT's policy, which prohibits community policing from handling

[21] When cases are concluded in the *circulo* rather than forwarded to the police station this is usually, according to interviews and observations of case settlements, either because the case is viewed as too minor to be handled by the official system, or because the victims prefer to refrain from going through the cumbersome process of a court case and/or because the victims lack confidence in the police to take their case seriously, or because of fear of corruption by the police (i.e. offenders paying the police to be released).

[22] Torture during investigations is done using batons (*chamboko* in Mozambican Portuguese): the suspect is told to lie down and 'sleep' or made to lie down and 'sleep' if he refuses to do so voluntarily, with head facing down, and is then hit in intervals of 3-5 strokes in his buttocks until he tells for example where the stolen goods are, who he works with or where he has acquired the drugs he is carrying. According to my observations of how the sector police officers operate this practice and the language used around it, the process is a clear imitation of the state police.

criminal cases and from using any kind of physical force: persons caught in the act of committing crimes are supposed to be immediately forwarded to the nearest police station or the officer present in the *bairro* (MINT 2005). Moreover, the principles of MINT's community policing policy starkly contradict the community policing agents' acquisition of handcuffs and batons. However, if this represents the official policy of the Ministry, practice is an entirely different matter. In fact, the state police have themselves partly contributed to the manner of local evolution of community policing.

Some of the instruments of force, batons and handcuffs, were originally granted to the community policing council by the state police, whereas others have been acquired by the young agents themselves. According to the community policing agents, some of them were also trained in 2003 by the state police in the use of the instruments, being instructed, for example, such as where and how to hit criminals with the baton, namely in the buttocks "so that the person does not have any clear marks or start to bleed".[23] At a meeting in 2009 with the police commander of the nearest police station, the community policing agents were also promised that they would soon receive new training sessions in the use of the instruments. The local ranks of the state police also frequently engage the community policing agents in their daily work. When the sector police officer is on duty in the *circulo,* he takes charge of the hearing of cases and makes the decisions as to whether they should be forwarded to the police station. At the same time he relies on the agents to help arrest suspects, collect information, notify suspects to appear at the police station, and to assist him during hearings at the *circulo*. On several occasions in 2009 the community policing agents also received orders from the nearest police station to search for or issue summonses to suspects on their own. All the agents are well-known at the police station, because they often accompany suspects, handcuffed, to the station – sometimes with and sometimes without a police officer. In fact, when the sector police officer or community policing agents call the station for assistance, it is very seldom that a police vehicle or uniformed officers on foot come to collect criminals caught *in flagrante*.[24] Moreover, the police station has on different occasions required the community policing agents to assist the police in nocturnal patrols, both on foot and using vehicles. It has also happened twice that the agents have been required to participate in searches for suspects directed from the police station.

[23] Interview, Community Policing Agent, Maputo, May 2009.

[24] During the entire period of my fieldwork in 2009 it only happened twice that a police vehicle came to pick up criminals at the *circulo*.

In short, the state police have come to rely extensively, yet unofficially, on the community policing agents in *bairro A* to do what officially are state police jobs. Importantly, they not only rely on them for assistance, but also quite extensively outsource police functions and instruments of force to them. In *bairro A* such outsourcing even includes the taking of measures that are now illegal for police officers. For example, on several occasions during 2009 the sector police officer ordered the community policing agents to beat suspects during investigations in the room of the *circulo*.

The relationship that has developed between the local state police and community policing in *bairro A* seems to be an inverted version of the rural situation described above: rather than using the legal plural situation to domesticate existing non-state institutions and thereby to reclaim a state monopoly on the handling of crimes and the use of force, the urban police officers outsource their functions and seem to share their monopoly with the 'new' community policing agents. However, from the perspective of the local police the practice of 'shared sovereignty' is acceptable only to the extent that the police are in control, and as long as it confirms the overriding authority of the state police. In other words, while the physical acts are outsourced, the monopoly to authorise them is not. In fact, outsourcing is not necessarily contradictory to, but can be seen as an element of police officers' efforts to boost their authority and improve the effectiveness of their work.

From the perspective of the sector police officer, the community policing agents have contributed significantly to his capacity to tackle cases and identify criminals, "because they [the community policing agents] are citizens of the *bairro* and they know the people there".[25] The manpower of the community policing agents is also important to him, because being only one officer to do patrols and arrest suspects in the *bairro* can be very risky for his personal security. Having a group of young men to escort him boosts his authority to act on crimes. For the police station the community policing agents are also considered to be the *de facto* extended arm of the state police and as contributing significantly to a reduction in crime levels.[26]

However, outsourcing is also a tricky business for the police, and the relationship between the state and the community police is ambiguous. One reason is that the

[25] Interview, Sector Police Officer, Maputo, April 2009.

[26] Interview, Police Commander in Chief, Maputo, June 2009.

police are often absent from the *bairro*, and when they are the community policing agents continue to do police work. They do so by essentially mimicking the practices and language of state police officers. This includes the detailed practices around hearings and investigations (how they sit on the chair, how they speak to the parties in a case, how they jot down names and ID details of persons when recording cases, how they use the baton and so forth). It also covers the use of state police titles (e.g. 'commander', 'chief of operations', 'patrol officer'). Moreover the community police have their own separate book for case records, including both the cases that are concluded by them and those that end up being forwarded to the police station. Much like the chiefs in Sussundenga, the community police also make reference to state police authority as a means to enforce sanctions, usually in the form of a threat to take suspects or criminals caught *in flagrante* to the police station.

The community policing agents in other words often take matters into their own hands, *de facto* acting as a local police force, and, while they draw on state police authority, they often refrain from informing the police about the crimes they handle. On several occasions in 2009 this led to tense discussion with the sector police officer, but, although he told the agents off, he did not explicitly complain about the community police to his superior. The crux of the matter is that the police need the community policing agents to improve their work, but also recognise that their authority to control crime is weakened when they outsource functions to the community police. The community police agents also know things about the police officers that would harm them if made public or if they reached their superiors, such as frequent incidents of police corruption like the extraction of 'tributes' from arrested persons to avoid prosecution. These intricacies of the relationship inform ongoing negotiations over who has the authority to decide cases and distribute information. There are many covert games played around case-handling.

Ultimately, state police authority over community policing is highly precarious, This, I suggest, in turn reflects overlapping layers of authority in the *bairro*. When explicitly asked, the community policing agents say that they have to follow the orders of the sector police officer and ultimately the commander in chief. The authority they themselves derive from being related to the police, as noted above, is also important. However, on a daily basis, it is actually the so-called 'structure of the *bairro*' (*a estrutura do bairro*) or what sometimes is referred to locally as the 'community' (*a comunidade*), which tends to assume authority over the community policing agents. This 'structure' or 'community' encompasses not the entire population, as envisioned by MINT's policy, but the *secretário do bairro* – the local state administrator – the Secretary of the Frelimo party branch in the *bairro*, and the group of people around these two figures: the *chefes dos quarterões* (the leaders of the different sub-sections of the *bairro*), the Frelimo women's organisation, and other members of the local Frelimo committee. In short, it is composed of the persons who represent and promote the interests of the ruling party, Frelimo. I now turn to consider how the specific politics of this structure have encompassed community policing.

Community policing agents as 'security agents' and 'sons of Frelimo'

The community policing organisation is integrated with the party-state structure of the *bairro* in various respects. In the area of conflict resolution and policing, it can be seen that there is a certain division of labour between the community policing agents, who handle crimes – at times with the state police – and the *secretário do bairro* who has charged himself to solve various 'social problems' (*problemas sociais)*.[27] The cases defined locally as 'social problems' range from non-criminal cases such as sorcery, conflicts over household plots, marital disputes, and conflicts between neighbours, to actual criminal cases such as domestic violence and rape. The *secretário* hears such cases on a daily basis, when people come by with particular problems or when problems are brought to him by the community policing agents or by one of the *chefes das quartarões*. These *chefes* form part of a semi-official system of *bairro* leadership, which is a residue of the old party-state structures. While this system is fully authorized by the local levels of the state, it has no *de jure* place in current laws on local state administration. The *chefes das quartarões* are all members of Frelimo, as is the *secretário* himself. They perform administrative functions and solve minor disputes between residents of their respective *quartarões* and forward more difficult cases to the *circulo* (hosting the *secretário,* the community police, the state police and the Frelimo party). The *chefes das quartarões* are also active participants in ruling-party activities and have a number of administrative duties.

---

[27] It should be noted that the *bairro* does not have a community court or any traditional authority to handle such conflicts. This absence cannot be generalized for the suburbs of Maputo. The neighboring *bairro* has for example recently set up a community court and some more semi-urban areas of Maputo also have traditional authorities.

While not everyone interviewed among the residents of *bairro A* stated that they in fact took their problems to their *chefe da quarterão* or to the *circulo* as a conflict resolution arena of first instance, there is a general agreement that this is the official procedure. It is then up to the *secretário* to decide where the case should be heard. The *secretário*'s role of distributing litigation is accepted by the community policing coordinator, Dona Sabina. The *secretário* also at times give a hand in solving those crimes that the community police are unsure about. However, disputes at times also arise between who should handle a case. Such was a case of domestic violence in mid-2009: the *secretário* first decided the case, but without his knowing the community policing agents then took over the case when the offender accused his wife of theft. In this case, the *secretário* intervened to assert his role as the final arbitrator, but there are also situations where the case ends with the police or remains disputed. When more serious disagreements over case-settlement responsibilities occur, including with the state police, the Frelimo secretary is also called in to discuss the matter. He takes the side of the '*bairro* structure'. This role of the local branch of the Frelimo party also extends beyond issues related to disagreements over jurisdictions, however.

The *secretário* and the Frelimo Secretary also have the role of approving new members of the community police, together with the *chefes das quartarões* and other key members of the ruling party. Moreover, if the coordinator fails to bring into line community policing agents who misbehave, it is this 'structure' that takes over. Given the strong role of the ruling party, it is therefore perhaps no coincidence that the coordinator herself, Dona Sabina, has a life-long history, in recent years as an active Frelimo *camarada* (comrade) in the women's league and before that in the popular vigilante organisation of the socialist regime. When not coordinating community policing she is also active in Frelimo party activities. Often she wears Frelimo t-shirts or caps when engaging in case-resolution at the *circulo*. Her right hand, the leader of the young agents below her, also happens to be a son of the Frelimo Secretary. Thus there is a strong overlap between the ruling party and the community policing organisation. This is reinforced by the fact that the *circulo* itself is the headquarters of the Frelimo party in the *bairro*. According to the *secretário,* the *circulo* is simply "lent out" to the community police and the state (the police and administration), because they lack their own venues. However, during the 2009 election campaign no one could doubt that the *circulo* was the 'house' of Frelimo: it was plastered with Frelimo election posters and blossomed with election-related activities.

The absorption of community policing, and one may say of 'legal pluralism' in general, under the roof of the ruling party has historical reasons. It can be seen as a residue from the socialist party-state era prior to 1990 when all powers were legitimately under the same roof. In Dona Sabina's words community policing "is just a new name for popular vigilantes. We do the same things as we did then", that is, not only providing security, but also, as the vigilantes did, defending the interests of Frelimo against opposing forces in society, or 'internal enemies' as such forces were named in the past (including both criminals, disturbers of public order and political opponents). Nonetheless, while history certainly informs present appropriations of community policing, the shared official discourse among the community policing agents, the Frelimo secretary and the *secretário*, was that policing was apolitical and could not serve political interests. They also share the view that "any person from any political party can become a member of the community policing". At the same time community policing agents also hold that it will probably be problematic if an agent does not sympathize with Frelimo or, worse, shows sympathy for another party. Thus the *de facto* inclusion of community policing under the field of authority of the party, I suggest, has less to do with ignorance of the principles of the democratic transition than with efforts to consolidate local ruling-party power. This was all the more explicit during the 2009 election campaign.

Shortly before the official campaign began, the community policing agents were strongly encouraged by their coordinator to sign up as members of the party so that they could acquire Frelimo membership cards. They were also invited to campaign-planning meetings where they were given stickers, posters and, importantly, food and drink. During the campaign itself the community policing agents were used as the 'security guards' of the campaign brigades (*brigadas da campanha*), when these did door-to-door visits, set up posters and otherwise delivered their messages in public. This work was not voluntary, but based on orders received from the coordinator and the *secretário*. In exchange the agents received tea and a big lunch every day – not unimportant for otherwise non-salaried agents.[28] While the agents complained to me that their police work was

[28] Membership of the community policing organisation is considered voluntary and carries no benefits such as subsidies, salary or contributions in kind. The issue of subsidies to community agents is a hot topic of discussion, also beyond *bairro A*, and lack of subsidies is widely considered one of the reasons why community policing has not been sustainable in many areas of the country. However, MINT strictly maintains the idea that community policing should be voluntary, based on the initiatives and communal interests of local citizens to improve the security

compromised by their role in the campaign, and some also subtly demonstrated reluctance when it was their turn to accompany the brigade, they felt that they had no choice but to be the 'security agents' of the party. They also repeated to me that "we are not involved in the politics of the party...we are just there to ensure security and order when the brigade walks around the *bairro*". When asked why they then did not accompany the brigades of the opposition parties, they were a bit unsure of what to answer, with one saying that "this *bairro* is all Frelimo so we do not do that" and another asserting that "we could do that but we were not asked to".[29]

The dilemma faced by the agents who claimed to be apolitical but found themselves being drawn into party politics was particularly felt during the last weekend of the campaign. Here the coordinator forced the agents to help to hang up Frelimo posters on private houses. While at first resisting the demand to participate, the son of the Frelimo Secretary later gave in and led a group of agents who ended up covering Renamo posters with Frelimo ones. This was accompanied by the chanting of Frelimo songs as they walked through the *bairro*. Having been initially reluctant, they suddenly were drawn into actively asserting a political role. While the association between Frelimo and the 'community' policing agents is only implicit during everyday police work, these overt political acts, bordering on the illegal, elicited overt criticism from local opposition party

---

situation of their area (personal communication, MINT functionary, May 2009).

[29] The state police was also involved in providing security to the larger campaign meetings of the Frelimo party during the run-up to the 2009 elections, as also in past elections. So in a sense the community policing agents' involvement can be seen as another area where they mimic the state police at a lower scale. The state police officers that I spoke with also held on to their apolitical role. They claimed that they did not provide security to other parties because the opposition party leadership had declined assistance from the state police. This discourse was also echoed in the national media, but at the same time there were various instances reported where the state police was accused of turning a blind eye to situations where Frelimo youth violently destroyed opposition party materials or blocked opposition campaigns, while arresting opposition party members who did the same or who were innocent. The similarity between state police and community police involvement in the election campaign, I suggest, points to a strong, historically-embedded tendency for the politicisation of policing in Mozambique (see Kyed 2007b, 2007a).

supporters. A young opposition party member reacted immediately, and shouted aloud in public that the community policing agents had no right to cover the Renamo posters: "We are living in a democracy...the police has no right to destroy the campaign of other parties", he shouted. He then managed to mobilise a small group of men who turned up in front of the *circulo* shouting their opposition. However, no one at the *circulo* took them seriously. Instead the women of the Frelimo brigade began to sing party songs facing the Renamo members, and the men told the Renamo members to be quiet and leave. The *secretário* told me that he did not want to engage in any resolution of the conflict, because "these Renamo people are not serious...they are thieves and drunk people whom Renamo has mobilised to create problems...to disturb public order". Similarly, some of the community policing agents, while agreeing that it was wrong to provoke Renamo, claimed to me that "those Renamo people are just angry because they are thieves, whom we have punished before". One agent also warned that if the Renamo members did not stop creating confusion, they would eventually be arrested for "physical aggression".

What these comments suggest is not only that the community policing agents are defending their own (*de jure* illegal) acts against the opposition in the local arena by referring to the latter as criminals. They reflect a much deeper political discourse that equates the political opposition with crime and disorder, that is, a discourse that characterises the opposition as the significant other of the 'good' community and of public order (Mouffe 2006: 18-19). The implication for the notion of legal pluralism, officially signifying diversity, is not simply a party politicisation of the newer kinds of urban 'community' policing and justice enforcement, e.g. as a means to gain votes. It also means that the plurality pertaining to actors that engage in conflict resolution and the handling of crime is overridden by efforts to monopolise the whole realm of public order(ing) by the ruling party. In this sense the real sovereign here is not the state, represented by its executive arm, the police, but ultimately the ruling party, which tends to (still) absorb the state.

Although the state police do indeed play a role in *bairro A* and are regarded as a significant authority, the day-to-day regulation of policing is in the hands of the ruling party, and more importantly, the party is the ultimate reference point of law and order. This is materialised in the *circulo* itself – the house of Frelimo under which roof all other authorities are housed. The local branch of the Frelimo party furthermore lays claim to *the* community – the community being those people who are organised around the party. This claim remains subject only to the weakest contestation in *bairro A*, as reflected by the opposition voiced by the Renamo members on the last weekend of the elections.

Having said this, I note that local contestations over the control of community policing have indeed occurred in *bairro A*, and there has been criticism of the ways in which community policing agents operate.[30] However, the role of the ruling party remains largely unquestioned in these contestations, which have mainly centred on individual leadership disputes. For example, when in 2007 the community policing council ceased to function, this was, according to various accounts, a result of internal leadership disputes among Frelimo members. Initially this led to the formation of parallel groupings of community policing agents, each performing patrols without being coordinated together from the *circulo*. By 2009 these agents had ceased to function, but one former member of the council was still trying to recapture his position against Dona Sabina who had won the internal dispute in 2007 by pitting the other members against the *secretário*. According to this former member, she had succeeded in doing this by spreading a rumour that he was secretly a supporter of Renamo. Thus party political discourse merges with the politics of local contestations over the control of community policing.

Conclusion

Legal pluralism as a *policy concept* can easily become subject to political manipulation or be a political tool to assert authority and manifest power by local state officials, local party cadres and, by extension, the national government. As shown in this article, the *politics of legal pluralism* is not, however, within the exclusive purview of state institutions attempting to assert authority over the non-state domain, although this element is very important. Local appropriations of legal pluralism or reactions thereto can also spark new forms of local contestations over authority or exacerbate existing ones. This may particularly be the case if

[30] For example in late 2009 one community policing agent was accused by a female resident of having beaten her son in public. This case is pending a court trial. In interviews with residents, frequent criticism was heard of the abuse of power by community policing agents, such as their arrests of innocent people and their extraction of money for their 'services'. This article does not address local residents' views of community policing in more detail because survey and qualitative data on these views have only recently been collected.

legal pluralism policies involve the setting up of new non-state institutions, such as community policing groups, or the revitalization of old forms of hybrid institutions, such as the community courts and village secretaries, alongside 'old' providers, such as chiefs. However, contestations may also occur because the reality often is that state and non-state institutions make competing claims to sovereignty, even though they at the same time may rely on conflicting norms and conceptions of justice. The histories of state engagement with non-state justice providers and their relationship to political configurations in the past, such as community court judges' relationship to the ruling party, equally affect the ways in which policies of legal pluralism are appropriated in practice.

It is of the utmost importance, I suggest, to consider the *politics of legal pluralism* in studies of legal pluralism policies, as well as in international efforts to support state recognition of non-state legal orders. At the heart of the issue is that justice enforcement, and by extension social ordering, are not neutral, apolitical activities, but political ones: they provide a route to authority and also often an income. For this reason, the different actors, state and non-state, referred to in policies as 'legal systems', seldom co-exist peacefully or without some degree of competition. The people who hold positions in them or whose interests are served by them will usually fight to maintain their power and positions. Thus, while policies on legal pluralism can be instances of state law adapting to local socio-cultural norms, they are bound also to involve elements of re-ordering of authority and power. This is partly fuelled by competing claims to authority:

> Groups or actors who benefit from, have a stake in, represent, or give rise to, the institutional structures of competing normative systems ... will defend and exert the power of their particular system in situations of a clash, not only because of their genuine commitment to and belief in the system, but also because their interests, identities, status and livelihoods are linked to it. (Tamanaha 2008: 400)

Moreover, it is important to acknowledge the asymmetrical power relations that inhere in the coexistence and recognition, of multiple legal orders. This is not a new phenomenon, nor is its observation new, but harks back to pre-colonial, colonial and earlier post-colonial encounters. For historical reasons state and non-state legal orders are not inherently distinct 'systems' that cater for separate spheres of social ordering, but rather clusters of rules, norms and institutions that have evolved together, albeit through an often ambiguous relationship of interdependence, competition and appropriation. At least as far as local level appropriations are concerned, current policies on legal pluralism can be expected to further create a situation of various degrees of merger and intermix.

As shown by the Mozambican case, new forms of plurality are, however, likely to co-exist with, and be reshaped by, state and regime efforts to monopolise the legal domain or to embrace pluralism, even to such an extent that the very notion of 'pluralism' itself comes under attack. This is reflected on the one hand in efforts to hierarchically subordinate non-state legal orders to state law and the overriding authority of state institutions, an objective often referred to in the literature as "weak legal pluralism" (Griffiths 1986). In Mozambique this is exemplified by state police attempts to reclaim sovereign authority by using state recognition to domesticate traditional authorities and by forms of controlled outsourcing of functions to young community policing agents. On the other hand, and a great deal more controversially, the notion of pluralism may be undermined by overt partisan political interests. In Mozambique this is exemplified by ruling party attempts to dominate 'old' non-state institutions, and to use 'new' non-state forms to expand and consolidate its power base. In the name of 'pluralism' the ruling party tries to monopolise the entire domain of public ordering and the notion of community. In everyday practice this not only considerably undermines the official state-authorised spaces for pluralism, but also seems to be much more difficult to contest than the claims to sovereign authority made in the name of the state.

The *politics of legal pluralism* described in this article may be more prevalent or explicit when there is no clear legal framework for interrelations between state and non-state providers or where no monitoring mechanisms are in place to ensure that local state officials adhere to an overriding set of rules on the manner of their engagement with non-state institutions. In fact, as I have suggested, the very lack of a clear legal framework may even be the product of political interests in the first place, as it more amply allows for political manipulation at the local level. However, even when we find a legal framework in place, it is still necessary to consider how this framework can be implemented and by whom. If implementation is left in the hands of local police officers, local court judges or local party-state actors, a range of manipulations can be expected to occur, precisely because of the inherent politics of justice provision and order enforcement. Representative councils or committees that include relevant state officials, non-state justice providers, civil society organizations and ordinary citizens could be a way to ensure check-and-balance mechanisms that would support equal access to justice and prevent political manipulation. Equally important are continued efforts to reform politically partisan and under-resourced official law enforcers, such as the police, who with few exceptions are *the* representatives of the formal system outside of towns and semi-urban administrative capitals. However, any efforts to address legal pluralism policies must also go to the root of the political in a given context, namely the wider political contestations and forms of organisation that go far beyond the 'legal domain' or the justice and security sectors.

As I have suggested, the politics of legal pluralism can be studied from the viewpoint of at least three layers of politics, but this may be expanded depending on the context in question. Thus we may consider: the politics of asserting the superior authority of state institutions and law over other existing legal orders or through the establishment of new non-state institutions; the political party interests in controlling non-state legal orders to consolidate power; and the politics of local level contestations over power and 'clients' to sustain the authority of a given institution or of specific personal power positions. These layers of politics may be partly overlapping in concrete actions, and they may be pitted against each other, such as when attempts by state actors to assert sovereign authority are contested by non-state actors in everyday dispute resolution. Irrespective of the layers of politics identified, it is important to study the consequences of legal pluralism as a 'policy concept' from an empirical perspective, and to critically scrutinize official policy claims and the often stereotypical descriptions of non-state legal 'systems' that inform such claims. Policies are informed by political power interests, and this is no less the case when these are formulated in the name of 'plurality' or 'the legal'.

References

BENDA-BECKMAN, Franz von, Keebet von BENDA-BECKMAN and Anne GRIFFITHS (eds.)
2009 *The Power of Law in a Transnational World.* New York-Oxford: Berghahn.

BUUR, Lars and Helene M. KYED
2006 'Contested sources of authority: re-claiming state sovereignty and formalizing traditional authority in post-conflict Mozambique.' *Development and Change* 37/4: 847-869.

2007 *State Recognition and Democratization in Sub-Saharan Africa. A New Dawn for Traditional Authorities?* New York: Palgrave.

DANIDA

2009 *Democratisation and Human Rights for the Benefit of the People. Strategic Priorities for Danish Support for Good Governance.* Copenhagen: Danish Ministry of Foreign Affairs, Danida.

DFID

2004 *Non-State Justice and Security Systems*. London: DFID.

GRIFFITHS, John

1986 'What is legal pluralism?' *Journal of Legal Pluralism* 24: 1-50.

HANDLER, Richard and Jocelyn LINNEKIN

1984 'Tradition, genuine or spurious.' *Journal of American Folklore* 97: 273-289.

ICHRP (International Council for Human Rights Policy)

2009 *When Legal Worlds Overlap: Human Rights, State and Non-State Law.* Geneva: ICHRP.

KYED, Helene M.

2007a *State Recognition of Traditional Authority. Authority, Citizenship and State Formation in Rural Post War Mozambique*, PhD dissertation. Roskilde: Roskilde University.

2007b 'The politics of policing: re-capturing 'zones of confusion' in rural post-war Mozambique.' Pp. 132-151 in Lars Buur, Steffen Jensen and Finn Stepputat (eds.), *The Security Development Nexus. Expressions of Sovereignty and Securitization in Southern Africa*. Uppsala: Nordic Africa Institute; Pretoria: HSRC.

2009a 'Traditional authority and localization of state law: the intricacies of boundary making in policing rural Mozambique.' Pp. 40-59 in Steffen Jensen and Andrew M. Jefferson (eds.), *State Violence and Human Rights*. Cavendish: Routledge.

2009b 'Community policing in post-war Mozambique.' *Policing and Society* 19/4: 354-371.

KYED, Helene M. and Lars BUUR

2006 'New sites of citizenship. recognition of traditional authority and group based citizenship in Mozambique.' *Journal of Southern African Studies* 32/3: 563-582.

MINT (Ministry of the Interior)

2005 *Policiamento Comunitário e Serviços Provinciais de Bombeiros, Reunião com os Municípios*. Manica, 25-27 July 2005 (unpublished paper).

MOMMSEN, Wolfgang and Jaap de MOOR (eds.)
1991 *European Expansion and Law: the Encounter of European and Indigenous Law in 19th and 20th Century Africa and Asia*. Oxford and New York: St. Martin's Press.
MOORE, Sally F.
1978 *Law as Process. An Anthropological Approach*. Hamburg: Lit Verlag; Oxford: James Currey.
1986 *Social Facts and Fabrications: 'Customary' Law on Kilimanjaro 1880-1980*. Cambridge: Cambridge University Press.
MOUFFE, Chantal
2006 *On the Political*. London and New York: Routledge.
OECD/DAC
2007 *Handbook on Security System Reform (SSR): Supporting Security and Justice*. Paris: OECD.
OOMEN, Barbara
2005 *Chiefs in South Africa. Law, Power and Culture in the Post-Apartheid Era*. Oxford: James Currey; Pieter Maritzburg: University of KwaZulu-Natal Press; New York: Palgrave.
REPUBLIC OF MOZAMBIQUE
2004 *Constituição da República*. Maputo: Imprensa Nacional de Moçambique.
2007 *Boletim da República, Lei 24/2007*. Maputo: Imprensa Nacional de Moçambique.
SANTOS, Boaventura de Sousa
2006 'The heterogeneous state and legal pluralism in Mozambique.' *Law and Society Review* 40/1: 39-75.
SERRA, Carlos (ed.)
2008 *Linchamentos em Mocambique,* Vol. I. Maputo: Eduardo Mondlane University Press.
TAMANAHA, Brian Z.
2000 'A non-essentialist conception of legal pluralism.' *Journal of Law and Society* 27/2: 296-321.
2008 'Understanding legal pluralism: past to present, local to global.' *Sydney Law Review* 30/3: 375-411.
TRINDADE, João C. and Boaventura de Sousa SANTOS
2003 *Conflito e Transformação Social. Uma Paisagem das Justiças em Moçambique*. Porto: Edições Afrontamento.
UNDP/WOJKOWSKA, Ewa
2006 *Doing Justice: How Informal Justice Systems Can Contribute*. Oslo: UNDP Oslo Governance Centre.

WEST, Harry G.
2005 *Kupilikula. Governance and the Invisible Realm in Mozambique*. Chicago: The University of Chicago Press.
WEST, Harry G. and Scott KLOECK-JENSON
1999 'Betwixt and between: "traditional authority" and democratic decentralization in post-war Mozambique.' *African Affairs* 98: 455-484.
WOODMAN, Gordon R.
1998 'Ideological combat and social observation: recent debate about legal pluralism.' *Journal of Legal Pluralism* 42: 21-59.
WORLD BANK
2008 *Forging the Middle Ground: Engaging Non-State Justice in Indonesia*. Washington: World Bank.

FARMERS' USE OF THE COURTS IN AN ANTI-LAND ACQUISITION MOVEMENT IN INDIA'S WEST BENGAL

Kenneth Bo Nielsen

Introduction[1]

In July 2006 a series of notifications for the acquisition of approximately 1,000 acres of agricultural land in an area known as Singur were served by the Communist-led Left Front Government (LF) of the Indian state of West Bengal. The acquired land in Singur would be converted into an industrial park and - as part of the LF's policy of revitalising the state's ailing industrial sector (Nielsen 2010) - leased out to Indian multi-national Tata Motors, who planned to set up a manufacturing unit that would produce the Tata Nano, the world's cheapest car. The notifications were issued under the Land Acquisition Act of 1894, the legislation under which land acquisition takes place in India.[2] This Act allows the

[1] Earlier versions of this paper were presented at the 'Legal Pluralist Perspectives on Development and Cultural Diversity' conference in Zürich in September 2009, and at a seminar at the Centre for Development and the Environment in Oslo the same month. I am grateful for the valuable input provided by the participants at both venues, particularly Susanne Brandtstädter, Dan Banik, Christopher Wright and Guro Aandahl. A special thanks to Stig Toft Madsen for his careful reading of an earlier draft; and to Gordon Woodman for encouraging me in bringing the paper into a publishable shape.

[2] See Khasnabis (2009) for an account of the evolution of land acquisition acts in India under colonial rule. In post-colonial India every state has the right to amend

government to exercise its right of eminent domain and acquire any land it sees fit, provided that it abides by certain provisions in the said Act. In accordance with these provisions Singur's project affected population, which included many small and marginal farmers (Banerjee 2006: 4719), were offered financial compensation for their losses.[3] But while some accepted cash in lieu of land a sizeable segment of local land owners did not. These so-called 'unwilling farmers' - i.e. land owners who refused to give their consent to the government's planned acquisition - organised a movement to protect their farmland. This movement has, in its struggle against the land acquisition, made use of a broad repertoire of contention that has, as I show below, included various forms of public action, contestation and negotiation. Importantly, the farmers and their supporters have also devoted significant time, energy and resources to challenging the land acquisition in both the Calcutta High Court (HC) and the Supreme Court of India (SC).

My aim in this article is to analyse *how* and *why* Singur's unwilling farmers have accessed and made use of the courts with such zeal in their opposition to the state-led expropriation of their farmland. What were their expectations from the court? Why did their court case challenging the land acquisition gain a special significance for them during certain phases of their movement? And how did the HC and SC respond to the unwilling farmers' petitions? The explanatory empirical account I present here is in the form of a largely descriptive chronological narrative that is deeply informed by my own experience from several spells of fieldwork in the acquisition-affected areas of Singur between 2007 and 2009. It was my own personal curiosity that led me to enquire into the relationship between the farmers and the legal system. Before I left for fieldwork I was aware that much of the literature on unofficial law and legal fora in countries of the South,

the provisions of the Land Acquisition Act. There thus presently exists a good deal of inter-state variation with regard to the technical aspects of land acquisition proceedings (Guha 2007: 49).

[3] The compensation consisted of the estimated market value plus a 30 per cent solatium (compensation awarded for injured feelings as distinct from financial loss or physical suffering); a 10 per cent incentive offered to those land owners, who agreed not to contest the acquisition; and 12.5 per cent interest (calculated for the period between the publication of the notification and the payment of the award) added to the estimated market value as a one-time amount. In cash terms the compensation for one acre of land in Singur was fixed at 840,000 Rupees for mono-crop land and 1,200,000 Rupees for multi-crop land (Nielsen 2008: 236).

including India, has often stressed the preference of local people for avoiding state law and courts, and for using their own more familiar fora instead. I knew this to be the case in West Bengal also where, according to political scientist Partha Chatterjee, many rural Bengalis *avoid* the law courts altogether as these are seen to be expensive, time-consuming, corrupt and insensitive to the specific demands of fairness in a particular case that only those intimately familiar with local histories and peculiarities could be expected to know (Chatterjee 2009: 43). And my immediate impression was that in this regard my study villages in Singur were no different. Litigation and going to court was socially frowned upon as it threatened to tear families apart, create mutual hostility, and to disturb the ostensibly 'harmonious' life of the village.[4] Instead, in times of conflict a peaceful and mutually acceptable solution would normally be sought through the intervention of a locally respected mediator who, having listened to all parties to the conflict, would propose an amicable compromise that would for the time being either solve the conflict or prevent it from escalating to socially unacceptable levels.[5] When I began conducting more in-depth interviews with unwilling farmers in Singur I also realised that many of them had, during the course of their movement to 'save the farmland', more often than not encountered the state's law enforcement agencies and the courts as sites of harassment and intimidation, not justice. Villagers had clashed with the police on several occasions, and hundreds of farmers had been beaten up, including women and the elderly. Many were hospitalised and some continue to suffer permanently from their injuries. Others had been arrested, many of them on false charges, including a two year old girl who was charged with rioting and imprisoned for four days. The many arrests kept movement activists busy raising money to bail the villagers out; and following their release on bail many farmers had regularly to travel many miles at their own expense to attend court hearings that usually produced only adjournments and more meetings. I was therefore surprised to find that some of Singur's unwilling farmers had not only decided to challenge the land acquisition in court, but that

[4] In practice, litigation over land, property or inheritance was not uncommon. Still, the discourse of 'the peaceful and harmonious village' provided an ideal model for rural life.

[5] Local mediators as a rule belonged to one of the two dominant political parties in the area. In West Bengal political parties have appropriated many if not most of the social institutions that mediate, and it is not uncommon to solicit a party's intervention in even the most intimate and private affairs (Bhattacharyya 2009: 60).

many more both keenly followed and attributed great importance to the fate of 'their' case in the HC.[6] If courts were generally shunned and not seen as sites of justice; and if other viable forms of contestation were available to them, why did they choose to repose faith in the ability of the law court to deliver justice?

The answer to this question is both complex and multilayered since, as I discovered after closely following the unwilling farmers' struggles for several years, the farmers did not *consistently* attach special importance to their court case. Rather, it was when other avenues of contestation and of seeking justice had either narrowed or closed entirely that the court case gained significance for the farmers. The courts were thus *one* among several available avenues through which justice could be sought, and the attractiveness of fighting one's case in court would therefore be highly context-sensitive and dependent on the utility of other available options at a given moment in time. Gaurang Ranjan Sahay provides an illustrative example of this dynamic, albeit on a much smaller scale. Sahay relates how in Bihar some members of the formerly untouchable *chamar* caste were beaten up by the Brahmins. A village level settlement was sought, but when it turned out that the case could not be settled here the *chamars* went to the police and the court for justice. However, when they realised that the court was not going to punish the Brahmins immediately, they beat some of the Brahmins up and withdrew the case (see Gupta 2009: 177-78). I argue here that Singur's unwilling farmers applied a similar logic of pursuing multiple paths to justice, including but not limited to going to court. I demonstrate the periodic waxing and waning of the farmers' interest in their case in the extensive empirical narrative that constitutes the second part of this paper.

Yet while the farmers thus believed that the court could *potentially* function as a dispenser of justice, i.e. by producing a verdict in their favour, they also suspected that it in reality functioned in rather unpredictable ways, and that going to court was somewhat of a gamble. The unwilling farmers expected that the court could be influenced and manipulated in a variety of ways, and that it would eventually rule as it pleased. Research from elsewhere in India suggests that legal arenas continue to "bend under the weight of the rupee or the stick" (Moore 1993: 539), and this clearly puts marginal and resource poor groups at a distinct disadvantage when

[6] A total of 11 petitions challenging the land acquisition had been filed in the HC. Yet the verdict would have consequences for all land losers in Singur, and the unwilling farmers therefore generally felt that this was 'their' case, and not the case of individual litigants.

confronting more powerful and influential actors such as state governments. Yet the perceived unpredictability of the courts, and the idea that courts would and could rule as they saw fit, also provided the Singur farmers with a sense of agency and hope: since the court was believed to be capable and likely to rule in an arbitrary fashion, one might just as well try one's luck even in the face of mighty opposition, and in spite of the fact that, as I show later, according to the letter of the law the unwilling farmers were always likely to lose.

To substantiate my argument that going to court is also seen as somewhat of a game of chance, I proceed below to examine some of the classical literature on the introduction and appropriation of British style legal systems and courts in India. Although much of this literature was produced in the 1950s and 1960s, the insights it generated remain relevant for an understanding contemporary India as well. The second section consists of the extensive empirical narrative on the unwilling farmers' use of the legal system, and in conclusion I return to address the questions raised in the introduction.

Games of Chance: Law and the Courts in India

The introduction of legal institutions in the Western mould gradually commenced with the arrival of colonial rule in India. The early trading of the East India Company was done from trading posts along the coast known as 'factories', and within those factories the British dispensed justice according to the law of England. The law empowering them to do so dates back to at least 1661 (Madsen n.d.). British colonial rule became increasingly consolidated during the second half of the 18th century, and by the late 18th century courts were being established in every district of British controlled India, with the procedure in court roughly based on existing procedures in British courts (Cohn 1961: 614). The intention underlying the establishment of such 'British' courts was to have available in India institutions designed to deal with issues related to the twin values that for the English more than anything defined a civilized people, namely the right to property and the rule of law (Metcalf 1998: 1).[7]

[7] According to Lloyd and Susanne Rudolph (1965: 24), having established the 'rule of law' on the Indian subcontinent was probably the proudest achievement of the British *raj* for most Englishmen. In addition, these new legal institutions were introduced with the aim of securing a full and regular collection of land revenue.

Several studies of the fate of these British style legal institutions in the Subcontinent have shown how their modus operandi were not immediately comprehended by those suddenly subordinated to their powers and influence. Most importantly, the jural postulates that underlie British procedural law and British-introduced courts - equality in the eyes of the law and judicial ignorance of the complainants; the idea that economic relations are based on contract rather than status; that the goal is to settle the case at hand and *only* that case; and that the purpose is to reach clear-cut decisions rather than compromises - were clearly at odds with a wide range of adjudication procedures followed in India's villages (Cohn 1988). This often caused confusion and conflict whenever the new British-style 'lawyer's law' met India's myriad local 'law-ways' at many level of society, such as in subdistrict and district courts, and in revenue and welfare offices and in the actions of the police. Yet the obvious lack of fit with indigenous jural postulates did not mean that the court as an *institutional* arrangement was rejected. On the contrary, many in the rural areas quickly learned to use the courts for their own ends, often with astuteness and effectiveness (Cohn 1965, 109) - but rarely as intended:

> Villagers use the courts for their own ends, and some villagers are adept at manipulating revenue, police, welfare, and judicial officials to minimize their effect on local institutions and affairs. To the villager, the rights and wrongs in a case were secondary to his ability to manipulate the court through access to minor court officials, the hiring of clever lawyers, the fabrication of evidence, and the marshalling of false witnesses. (Cohn 1965: 104-6).

The result was that the courts were flooded with cases which took years to resolve. This led to a huge backlog of cases, high costs of litigation (although there was no shortage of inexpensive lawyers), oppression of cultivators by those able to manipulate the legal system, and an endemic use of perjury and forgery of evidence and documents, official or otherwise (Cohn 1961, 622). Rather than settling disputes the courts were more often than not used as a form of gambling (Khare 1972, 78) on the part of legal speculators, who used them to wrest property from others. Apparently, the quickest way to ruin a rival - provided one was clever and lucky enough - was to run him into bankruptcy by embroiling him in a law suit (Cohn 1988, 568-9). As a result, rather than becoming dispensers of justice the courts in practice became variously arenas for harassment; places to gain revenge; battlegrounds in which to carry out fights to eliminate rivals; or fora where status and prestige could be won. With reference to North India, Cohn notes how:

> [a] wealthy Thakur [locally dominant caste of landlords] who went to court looked forward to not just one quick case, but to a series of cases, appeals, adjournments and counter appeals through which a poorer competitor could be ruined. Since British procedure appeared capricious to the Indians, someone with a bad case was as prone to go to court as someone with a good case. The standard was not the justice of his case, but his ability to outlast his opponents. (Cohn 1988: 573.)[8]

As a consequence, and although the British intended to bring 'justice' to the subcontinent, their legal system often produced results that were experienced as injustice (Rudolph and Rudolph 1965, 26). In the words of historian Percival Spear: 'the courts were to the public a great penny in the slot machine whose workings passed man's understanding and from which anything might come except justice' (quoted Cohn 1961: 622).

Yet the enthusiastic litigiousness[9] displayed by some - often locally dominant - social groups simultaneously made the law courts very unpopular, and success as a litigant did not necessarily translate into social status. Writing about the South Indian village of Rampura sociologist M. N. Srinivas found, based on fieldwork in the late 1940s, that local villagers felt that respectable people ought not to frequent the law courts. Srinivas' villagers opined that disputes were better settled in the village than in the law courts, which were a place one should only go when one had exhausted all other remedies.[10] Accordingly, those villagers who frequented

[8] Indeed, so successfully was the British style legal system appropriated that in Bengal already by 1815 'chicanery and litigiousness appear[ed] almost universally to have taken the place of violence' in revenue collection (the Marquess of Hastings, quoted Marshall 1987: 140).

[9] Rudolph and Rudolph (1965: 30), however, have suggested that the apparent rise in litigiousness at least partly reflected the transplantation of disputes to a new location, i.e. the law court, where they were more susceptible of statistical observation.

[10] Writing in the 1970s R. S. Khare (1972: 79-80) similarly argued that the first

the courts excessively were unpopular and had a reputation for being very unscrupulous. Srinivas also noted how much of what went on in a law court made absolutely no sense to the villagers: to them the most significant thing about a court case was that a clever lawyer had to be hired.[11] And when a man lost in a government law court it did not mean that he had done wrong or that he would lose face with his fellow villagers; it merely meant that his lawyer had not been clever enough, or that he had been unlucky: "Villagers know that a man who has a right to a thing may lose it in a law court and the man who has no right may win it" (Srinivas 1959: 14).

As mentioned courts in West Bengal are still widely perceived as corrupt, expensive and time-consuming (Chatterjee 2009: 43). In addition they tend to operate slowly. According to recent official figures from the home ministry's department of justice, nearly 30,000,000 cases are pending in various Indian courts (*Hindustan Times* 2007).[12] This ostensibly means, according to High Court Judge V V Rao, that even if the courts were to stop registering new cases and work only at disposing of the cases on hand, it would take 320 years for all cases - given the present size of the judiciary - to be disposed of (*The Times of India* 2010). In West Bengal alone, according to the state law minister, 1,940,000 cases are presently pending in the lower courts and an additional approx. 200,000 in the High Court (*The Statesman* 2006). Given this slowness of the legal system even a verdict in favour of Singur's unwilling farmers was likely to arrive too late, i.e. after the expropriation order had been carried out and their farmland converted into an industrial site. And lastly, and perhaps most importantly, the Land

popular reaction among Indians towards the British-style 'lawyer's law' was to shun it and avoid it as far as possible, and to seek morally and socially more desirable informal settlements and out-of-court compromises instead.

[11] Elsewhere Srinivas writes:

> The villagers did not understand the law or justice which was dispensed in [the law courts]. The legal system appeared to many as a complicated and half-understood game which litigants played by hiring lawyers who were supposed to know the rules. (Srinivas 1980: 114.)

[12] Even more recently, *The Times of India* (2010) reported that the number of pending cases stood at 31.28 million. According to official estimates it takes 15 years on average to finally decide a court case in India (*Hindustan Times* 2010).

Acquisition Act of 1894 does in fact not contain any clause that gives any power to the affected people to prevent the acquisition (Guha 2007: 55), nor is the acquiring agency required to elicit the consent of those affected by the acquisition (Samaddar 2009: 154). Hence, people like Singur's unwilling farmers who seek to prevent or undo a proposed acquisition through the courts as a rule hardly ever win. Against this background the Singur farmers' recourse to the courts appears as a legal game of chance where the chance of winning was small – but not nil.

Resisting the Land Acquisition: From the Streets to the High Court

The unwilling farmers did not immediately take their grievance to court when they first learnt, in May 2006, that their land was targeted for expropriation. Instead they almost immediately organised to resist, and formed a committee - the Committee to Save the Farmland of Singur - to organise their protest movement. Under the committee's guidance a number of public demonstrations, rallies and meetings were held. Other forms of public action were undertaken as well, such as the blocking of railways and roads by movement activists. Attendance varied, but generally several thousand villagers participated. On several occasions the protestors adopted an aggressive and confrontational stance against visiting representatives of the LF and Tata Motors, and on more than one occasion demonstrations organised by the committee were met with police repression. The unwilling farmers' protests generated considerable media and public attention, and many urban NGOs, activist groups and political parties came out in support of the anti-land acquisition movement. This included most significantly West Bengal's leading opposition party the Trinamul Congress (TMC). The farmers' committee had as its president appointed the area's member of the state legislative assembly (MLA), who represented the TMC. In this capacity he brought the Singur issue to the attention of the TMC leadership, including its high-profile supreme leader Mamata Banerjee. Mamata Banerjee lent her full support to the unwilling farmers' movement and came down heavily on the LF for acquiring the land of small and marginal farmers without their consent. She also went on to consistently provide both political, logistic and financial assistance to the movement, and the entry into the protests of the TMC (and other organisations) propelled the Singur protests to the level of state- and nationwide politics. This generated significant public pressure on the LF to withdraw its land acquisition plans in Singur.

When I arrived in Singur for an extensive period of fieldwork in the latter part of 2007, some 16 months after the local protests had started, I interviewed unwilling farmers about their recollection of those early months of their movement, and almost without exception they remembered this as a time when they had felt confident that their agitation would force the LF to abandon its land acquisition in Singur and to relocate the Tata factory elsewhere. This, however, did not happen. After tolerating the Singur farmers' protests for several months the LF had gone ahead and acquired and fenced the land in December 2006 under heavy police protection. Shortly after it was handed over to Tata Motors, who soon began construction work on the site. Evidently, the unwilling farmers' many months of public protests and movement activities during 2006 had failed to generate the result they desired. So too had the farmers' committee's attempt at arriving at a mediated and negotiated solution. The committee had sent a number of deputations bearing petitions, memoranda and letters of protest to locally influential government bodies such as the block development officer (BDO) and district magistrate (DM). In their petitions the farmers expressed their opposition to the land acquisition, and implicitly urged local authorities to convey this opposition to those higher up in the system. Yet as the fencing of their land began in December 2006 it became apparent that these more 'traditional' attempts at dispute resolution by seeking to bring in locally influential people - the BDO or the DM - as mediators between themselves and the LF had failed.[13]

With both public protests and mediation having ostensibly failed in their objective the law court became an increasingly important arena for the unwilling farmers. Petitions challenging the land acquisition were filed already in 2006, and more followed in 2007. Some were filed by local farmers themselves with the help of legal experts provided by the TMC or by NGOs, while others were filed as public interest litigation by people and organisations sympathetic to the farmers' movement.[14] The many petitions were first heard by the HC in late December 2006, and subsequently hearings continued intermittently almost throughout 2007, particularly during July and August when hearings took place on 24 different

---

[13] According to Ranabir Samaddar this form of dispute resolution was never likely to produce any result that would have satisfied the unwilling farmers. It merely gave local movement leaders the honour of being invited to the DM's chamber, but there was in fact nothing the DM could do if the unwilling farmers did not fall in line (Samaddar 2009: 163).

[14] Any Indian citizen can bring any issue before the court if it is deemed to be in the public interest, i.e. regardless of whether the citizen in question has any *locus standi* in the traditional sense or not.

dates. Occasionally groups of farmers would make the one and a half hour train journey from Singur to the HC to witness the proceedings, although they understood next to nothing of what was being said as they were conducted in English.

While I cannot say with certainty how much importance the Singur farmers attached to the possibility of challenging the land acquisition in court during the early months of their movement, it is telling that of the 11 petitions filed in the HC, seven of them were not filed until 2007, i.e. *after* the land had been acquired and fenced. Evidently recourse to the court had become a more attractive option after the farmers' public protests had failed. And when I embarked on fieldwork in late 2007, it was obvious that the HC case had by then acquired a special significance. For the unwilling farmers prospects were bleak. It was nearly a year since the land had been acquired, and construction work inside the factory compound was well under way, with contingents of police and private guards providing a heavy security cover. The number of public protest rallies and demonstrations undertaken by the unwilling farmers had declined considerably, and many felt disenchanted that the many months of movement activities had not been enough to prevent the acquisition. Now they pinned their hopes on a favourable HC verdict instead. As if to emphasise the importance of the HC case, movement leaders, whom I interviewed at the time, sometimes referred to their movement as a 'legal movement', i.e. a movement which - in addition to obeying the laws of the land - sought justice through the legal system.[15] Likewise, during interviews with unwilling farmers, the interviewee would often and without my encouragement bring up the court case. And in public discourse and discussions the HC case figured frequently. This was especially so during village meetings organised by the farmers' committee. I had expected that these meetings would have devoted considerable time to organising and preparing for various forms of public protests (rallies, roadblocks etc.), but instead a comprehensive report on the progress of their case would normally be the first item on the agenda. The following excerpt from one such village meeting, held in November 2007, brings out the significance of the HC case in the eyes of the unwilling farmers at the time.

[15] On an earlier occasion movement activists had spent considerable time collecting sworn affidavits from some 800 unwilling farmers on official revenue stamp paper, with the explicit purpose of disproving the contents of a flawed status report on the Singur land acquisition prepared by the LF, in a manner that would stand up in court (Nielsen 2008: 237-8).

A village meeting

Some 45 villagers, mostly men, had gathered at around 10 pm on the porch of Mr Manna's house to attend a meeting convened by the local anti-land acquisition committee. It was a cold night and everybody was wrapped in blankets as they sat or squatted on the cool concrete floor of Manna's porch. The committee's president began by welcoming the villagers and thanked them for attending at this late hour. He then immediately proceeded to inform them about a verdict delivered by the HC only days ago in a case related to land acquisition and police atrocities in Nandigram elsewhere in West Bengal. Here the LF had tried to acquire some 14,000 acres of agricultural land for a chemical hub, but had later been forced, amidst violent local protests, to abandon the plan.[16] However, in one clash between villagers and the police many villagers had been killed or injured by police firing. The HC had ruled the firing unconstitutional and avoidable, and had ordered the LF to pay a significant compensation to the next of kin of those killed. In addition the bench had ordered compensation for those raped and molested. The president explained that this verdict was good news for the Singur farmers because Singur and Nandigram were comparable cases since they both concerned forced land acquisition. And so, if the HC had ruled in favour of Nandigram's farmers it should naturally do the same for Singur's farmers, the president opined. Besides, the lawyer Kalyan Bandyopadhyay, who had represented the people of Nandigram in the HC, was also representing the people of Singur in their case - and one would expect Bandyopadhyay's success in the Nandigram case to rub off on his performance in the Singur case as well. The president then added that Siddhartha Sankar Ray was also part of Singur's legal team. In addition to being an eminent lawyer Ray had, the president explained, been the chief minister of West Bengal many decades back, and had gone on to serve as the governor of Punjab and as India's ambassador to the United States: "Normally he will charge many *lakh*[17] to attend a hearing on behalf of his clients, but he has told me personally not to worry about his salary - he will represent us anyway", the president said. The assembled villagers nodded approvingly and appeared pleased at having such eminent lawyers on their side; and the fact that Ray found their case so deserving that he was willing to forego his fee was an added bonus.

[16] The events in Nandigram are described in Ray (2008).

[17] One *lakh* is 100,000 Rupees.

The president then brought up a recent case from Punjab, where a group of farmers had contested a land acquisition in the Punjab and Haryana HC. They had initially lost, but had subsequently taken their case before the SC, which had overturned the HC's verdict. The SC had found that good agricultural land should not be acquired for setting up factories, and that the state should always try to acquire only barren or waste land.[18] This ruling was good news for several reasons, the president explained. Firstly, since Singur's agricultural land was generally fertile and multi-crop, according to the SC ruling the LF should clearly have acquired less fertile land elsewhere. And secondly, even if the HC were to rule against the Singur farmers they could be confident that an appeal case brought before the SC would give them justice: "In the SC we are sure to win, because if the SC rules in favour of the farmers in the Punjab it will *have* to rule in favour of us as well", the president argued; "The SC is the SC of all of India, so naturally it has to speak with *one* voice. It cannot rule that something that is illegal in Punjab is legal in West Bengal. So in the SC we will surely win", he added. The villagers nodded enthusiastically in agreement, even as the president went on to explain that seeking justice through the legal system could be a long process: "No matter what, our case will go all the way to the SC, because if we lose in the HC we will appeal to the SC; and if the LF loses they will appeal." But as the Punjab case illustrated it would be worth the wait: "We can have confidence in the SC", the president concluded.

The president sat down and encouraged the committee's vice president Mr. Mukherjee to say a few words. Mukherjee was a supporter of a far-left Marxist-Leninist political formation, and, although he welcomed the verdicts on Nandigram and the Punjab, he also - in a more Marxist vein - cautioned the villagers against putting too much faith in the courts:

> The court has now produced some favourable verdicts, but it could have done more. It could have issued a stay on construction work on the factory while the case was pending, but it has not done so. To get a good verdict for us we cannot just lean back and relax. We need to keep up our movement activities, including big rallies, marches and demonstrations. This will show the people and the HC that we are keeping a close eye on the case and that we are still serious and angry. It will put pressure

[18] The SC had delivered its verdict in the Punjab case in October 2007. See Ray Choudhury (2008) for a brief report.

on the HC and make it difficult for them to rule in favour of the government.

Mukherjee sat down and a local village leader rose to speak. He too immediately mentioned the Singur farmers' case in the HC and said that he had heard from a friend of his, who often frequented the HC premises, that the lawyers there generally felt that the Singur farmers would win. Many lawyers also personally sympathised with the unwilling farmers, which was good news since they might be able to influence the judges assigned to the Singur case. He also reminded the audience of how the HC had previously embarrassed the LF by ruling that the prohibitory orders it had imposed on Singur in the wake of the actual acquisition of the farmland - to prevent the unwilling farmers from protesting in public - had been illegal.[19] This showed, he concluded, that the HC is not afraid of ruling against the government: "There is hope for us in the HC", he proclaimed. Thus assuaged the villagers rose and headed home.

The Letter of the Law and the HC Verdict

Evidently, by late 2007 a favourable HC verdict had become the unwilling farmers' main source of hope for getting their land back. Mukherjee's comment at the meeting shows that various forms of public action and protest had not been abandoned entirely, but it was clear that their function and purpose had changed: earlier demonstrations and protest rallies had been organised to force the LF to backtrack and undo its land acquisition. Now, ostensibly, they were conducted primarily to influence the HC. Yet when the HC delivered its verdict some two months after the village meeting described above it ruled *against* the farmers, and found that the LF had acted in accordance with the Land Acquisition Act of 1894. Before I discuss the HC verdict it is instructive to briefly introduce the key features of this Act.

[19] When it began acquiring the land in Singur the LF had imposed section 144 of the Code of Criminal Procedure, which it then extended several times. Section 144 specifies the authorities' power to issue order in urgent cases of nuisance or apprehended danger. In the Singur case the HC ruled that the state authorities had abused their power and violated citizen's rights when imposing section 144 (Prahladka et al. 2007).

The Land Acquisition Act of 1894 - essentially a colonial measure intended to ensure a smooth acquisition of land for mining, roads and railways, or irrigation works - empowers the state government, upon proper preliminary notification, to acquire land in any locality where such land is likely to be needed for any 'public purpose' or for a 'company' (Sarkar 2007: 5). The Act suggests what might qualify as a 'public purpose', but does not offer any definitions. With regards to the notion of 'company' there are some restrictions attached to acquiring land for a government company, while the acquisition of land for a private company is very restricted.

The acquisition begins when the collector issues a public notice to that effect. Those affected by the acquisition plans have the right to object to the District Collector, who is obliged to consider such objections before forwarding his final recommendations to the government. Once a final decision is taken by the government, the collector initiates the process of marking out and measuring the land, and announces that claims for compensation (the award) may be made to him (Sarkar 2007: 6-11). The market value of the land at the time of the publication of the notification 'shall be taken into account' when the award is fixed. Those affected by the acquisition can challenge for example the size of their award and the collector's measurement of their land by going to court (Sarkar 2007: 17-27). They can also refuse to accept the compensation altogether in which case it will be deposited with the court. But in reality there is no provision in the Act which allows the affected population to challenge the acquisition *per se*. Going to court can thus only delay the process or enhance the rate of compensation (Guha 2007: 55).[20]

In the HC it was the notions of 'private company' and 'public purpose' that

[20] The act has been criticised on many accounts. Nowhere does it provide for any compensation for those who till the land without having legal title, such as sharecroppers or labourers. It makes no mention of rehabilitation since as per the Act, the responsibility of the state towards those affected by the acquisition ends with the payment of compensation. Only individual property rights are recognised, whereas community rights over land are ignored so that if village commons are acquired, no compensation is provided (Guha 2007). In addition, a policy that reduces the value of land to a one-time monetary compensation is likely to be experienced as both problematic and unjust in a rural setting like Singur, where land to an extent retains its social and political value, even though the local economy today is by no means strictly agrarian.

emerged as the focal points of legal contestation. The farmers' legal team argued that the initial land acquisition notifications had been vague with regard to whether land was being acquired for a company or for a public purpose, to the extent that the notification could not be considered 'proper'. Yet in the team's opinion it was clear that, since the land in Singur, once acquired, would be leased out to Tata Motors, the entire land acquisition was *de facto* being carried out for or on behalf of a *private* company. This, they argued, meant that the LF had failed to abide by the appropriate provisions of the law. They added that the land acquisition was a scam done with malafide intentions to benefit Tata Motors. Yet the LF's legal team efficiently countered this charge by pointing out that technically it was the West Bengal Industrial Development Corporation (WBIDC) - the premier agency of the State's Commerce and Industries Department - which acted as the acquiring agency. Whatever the WBIDC subsequently did with the land was a moot point from the point of view of the law.

In contrast the notion of 'public purpose' proved more controversial. The key question was: does a car factory constitute a public purpose or not? When confronted with this question by the media the West Bengal Minister of Industries had replied: "of course it is a public purpose, industrialisation means employment generation, it means development of society. The entire people of the state will be benefited" (Nirupam Sen, quoted Chattopadhyay 2006). In the HC the LF's legal team maintained the public purpose nature of the Tata project. Industrial projects like the one in Singur would generate growth and employment that would benefit the entire state. This was true, the LF's lawyers argued, even if one *assumed* that the acquisition was for the benefit of a company: industries generated socio-economic development no matter what. The farmers and their advocates begged to differ. For them acquiring the land of small and marginal farmers by force only to lease it out - with considerable state subsidies[21] - to a private multinational could not be justified as a public purpose. They saw it rather as a kind of inverse Robin Hood where land was taken from the poor and gifted to the rich: thousands of farmers would lose their livelihood[22] because of the land acquisition, but only a

[21] According to one estimate, the car factory in Singur has been directly subsidised to the tune of 8.5 billion Rupees (Bidwai 2008: 117). The WBIDC provided Tata Motors with a 2 billion Rupees loan at a rate of one per cent; however, in order to extend the loan the WBIDC itself had to take a significantly more expensive loan from the market (Samaddar 2009: 171).

[22] More than 10,000 land owners were affected by the land acquisition in Singur.

few hundred well-educated engineers would find employment in such a hi-tech modern car factory. And Tata Motors would make all the profits. This, the farmers felt, did not qualify as a public purpose.

When the Court delivered its verdict in January 2008 it firstly dismissed more than half of the eleven petitions challenging the land acquisition as 'not maintainable', and treated the remaining petitions as 'almost identical' (Calcutta High Court 2008, 9). In its verdict the HC found:

> The materials placed before us do not lead to the necessary or even reasonable conclusion that the Government machinery identified itself with the private interests of the company, forsaking public interest. Public purpose does not cease to be so merely because the acquisition facilitates the setting up of industry by a private enterprise and benefits it to that extent.... On the face of it, therefore, bringing into existence a factory of this kind would be a purpose beneficial to the public even though it is a private venture. (Calcutta High Court 2008: 10-11.)

The HC in other words accepted the proposition that the land acquisition in Singur was legal insofar as it was carried out for a public purpose. It also dismissed the case from the Punjab - mentioned during the village meeting - as not having 'any bearings on the given facts of this case' (Calcutta High Court 2008: 14).

The defeat in the HC provoked an angry response from Singur's unwilling farmers, who almost immediately called rallies and organised road and railway blocks to show their resentment to the public. To explain the implications of the verdict the movement leadership organised another series of village meetings. Here they clarified that this was not really a defeat after all, since the case would have been appealed to the SC by one side or the other regardless of the HC's ruling. Besides, they explained, the HC was just a 'local court' and as such susceptible to manipulation by the powers that be, i.e. the LF. Having been in power in West Bengal since 1977, wasn't it likely that the LF had built up the capacity to meddle with the courts? one leader wondered out loud. One of the HC judges, another movement leader alleged, was 'close to the government', while the other was believed to be hand-in-glove with Tata, for whom he had ostensibly once worked as a corporate lawyer. That was the *real* reason why their petitions had been dismissed, the leader argued. But with the appeal case matters would be entirely different: the SC was the SC of *India,* and as such not entangled in local relations of power and dominance to the same degree; and here not even the immense political influence of the LF would be able to assert itself. As soon as their lawyers had had a chance to go through the HC's verdict they would begin putting together their appeal case, the leadership concluded. According to the leadership it was thus not that their legal team had argued their case poorly; nor that the letter of the law simply went against them – the problem was that their opponent, the LF, had simply played the legal game more efficiently in this instance.

It was my impression that in spite of the setback in the HC many villagers continued to repose faith in the ability of the SC to eventually deliver a verdict in their favour.[23] It would be an exaggeration to argue that the unwilling farmers conceived of the SC as akin to the an incorruptible and ideal Hindu king,[24] who ensures for his subjects *Ram Raja* (just rule) on earth; but to a number of unwilling farmers the SC did indeed appear as a distant and magnificent centre of power that could enforce justice and make even the powerful LF government comply with whatever it wished through a mere stroke of its pen. When I asked the unwilling farmers about their expectations from the SC many simply replied that: 'All we have to do is wait – our work is done'. By this, I believe, they meant that their long struggle for justice on the streets as well as in court was finally coming to an end. Now all they had to do was wait for a favourable SC verdict.

[23] The Indian SC has a reputation for being a people's court. The Constitution gives all Indians the right to petition the SC directly if their fundamental rights are violated and the right to appeal to it in many other cases. Yet from West Bengal a mere 1.7 percent of the cases heard in the HC are appealed, and of the cases relating to fundamental rights and public interest litigation heard by the SC, the SC has ruled increasingly over the last 30 years against the socially disadvantaged. Most of the cases the court decides are brought on appeal by those with money and power (Robinson 2010).

[24] The special quality of the ideal Hindu King is that he can never be corrupted. If for some reason justice does not prevail in his realm, or if true justice is not delivered, it is not because of any personal weakness or flaw on the part of the King. The problem rather would be the King's dishonest advisors and ministers who stand between the benign ruler and his subjects and poison his ear - in much the same way as corrupt officials, petty judges, dishonest state ministers, lower court clerks and dodgy lawyers stood between the Singur farmers and the benign SC.

Back to the Streets and Towards Elections

However, signs soon emanated that the SC might not entertain a munificent view of the Singur farmers' cause. In May 2008 the SC refused to stay the HC's order (Venkatesan 2008), and when hearings finally began in the SC in April 2010, the court was quick to proclaim - with reference to the 'company vs. public purpose' controversy - that even if a state were to acquire land for a *private* company, it could in fact serve a *public* purpose nonetheless (Rautray 2010). When this article went to press the hearings had not been concluded, but by now the importance of the SC's eventual verdict had long since decreased significantly for the Singur farmers, whose protests had taken a different turn in the wake of the unfavourable HC verdict. In the summer of 2008, some six months after their defeat in the HC, thousands of people began gathering daily outside Tata's now nearly completed car factory. Many locals joined in, but the majority of the participants were supporters of the TMC and other political parties, who were bussed in from elsewhere. Party leader Mamata Banerjee, who had by then made opposition to forced land acquisition one of her main poll planks, led the demonstration and demanded that Tata Motors return 400 acres of land from inside the factory compound to the unwilling farmers. After prolonged protests (and some failed negotiations) Tata finally relented and announced their departure from Singur. Chairman Ratan Tata said that it would be impossible for him to run a factory under such hostile local conditions in the long run, and accordingly ordered the factory dismantled and moved nuts and bolts right across India to the state of Gujarat. Tata's departure spawned cautious celebrations among Singur's unwilling farmers, and although they soon realised that Tata's withdrawal made little actual difference on the ground as the LF still refused to return any of the acquired land, it had demonstrated that the politics of the street and public agitation had now achieved what the court had not, namely to rid Singur of Tata Motors.

I arrived in Singur for a final round of fieldwork in early 2009, some months after Tata's departure. During my stay a new series of village meetings were held and the SC case figured only sparingly. The odd villager would inquire how the appeal case progressed, or would angrily wonder how much longer they would have to wait for a verdict. But neither the leadership nor most of the villagers showed any urgent interest in the case any more. Instead the talk was about the emergence of an entirely new political situation in the state, one in which their demand would in all likelihood be listened to and met. Since the Singur controversy erupted in 2006 the TMC had opposed the LF's policy of acquiring agricultural land for industrial purposes in a number of localities across the state, and had made the protection of agricultural land a major political issue. This had brought the TMC increasing support from voters at recent successive elections, including local level elections in Singur. With State Assembly elections just two years away, and with the political mood prevalent in the state apparently favouring the TMC, it looked likely that the TMC would be able to oust the LF from power. Were that to happen TMC leader Mamata Banerjee had promised to immediately undo the land acquisition in Singur and return 400 acres to its erstwhile owners. Accordingly, much of the movement leadership in Singur were now engaged in campaigning for the TMC in Singur and elsewhere, believing that they would get the land back if a TMC-led government assumed office in West Bengal in 2011. Rather than relying on the SC to force the LF to give up on Singur, removing the LF altogether through the ballot had now assumed top priority as the swiftest and most realistic route to reclaiming the land. In this endeavour the SC had lost its utility.

Conclusion

The account presented here shows how the courts can both gain and lose importance for subaltern groups in their pursuit of justice. For Singur's unwilling farmers, going to court constituted one part of a larger repertoire of contention which they made use of in their struggle to get their land back. From the outset they pursued the paths of confrontational street politics in combination with local mediation and negotiation, but when these failed to produce the desired result, the court assumed increasing importance as an arena of contestation. In accessing the court a host of allies, including political parties with money and connections, urban-based NGOs, and various legal experts providing free assistance, have been of crucial importance for the farmers.

The idea of the court as ideally a dispenser of justice was thus not alien to Singur's unwilling farmers. The speeches delivered by the movement leadership – and the reception of them by the villagers – testify to this. Importantly, the further removed from local relations of power and dominance the court was physically located, the higher the likelihood of being given 'fair treatment'. Thus, when the HC verdict went against them the farmers dismissed it as just a verdict from a local court that had been manipulated by the LF and Tata Motors – incidentally, the Calcutta High Court is located very close to the state assembly where the LF rules supreme,[25] and not very far from the headquarters of the LF's largest constituent, the Communist Party of India (Marxist). Hence, their chances were likely to improve when the case was brought in front of the powerful and autonomous SC in Delhi, the farmers felt.

The farmers' point of view that courts were susceptible to manipulation by the powers that be indicates that, while they believed the court *capable* of delivering a 'just' ruling in their favour, they did not automatically *expect* the court to do so. Going to court was also a game of chance, and while this provided the farmers with a sense of agency vis-a-vis the courts – they used various forms of public protest to 'put pressure' on it – it also meant that it would be naive to rely exclusively on the court when it came to reclaiming the land, particularly when their opponent ostensibly had more rupees and wielded a bigger stick. The farmers accordingly never abandoned the strategy of seeking a political rather than a legal solution to their predicament. For a while the politics of agitation was either subordinated to or enlisted in the service of seeking a solution through the court, but when suddenly the politics of agitation and the ballot, resurrected and spearheaded by the TMC, promised to provide a likelier and swifter return of their land than could the SC, the unwilling farmers gradually lost interest in their case, the outcome of which would be irrelevant.

While the empirical case presented here might not be paradigmatic, it shows that Indian courts do constitute an arena where subaltern groups can and do seek justice for themselves. From the point of view of subaltern agency it would be foolish – since the courts ostensibly rule in mysterious ways – not to bring one's case before them, even if one's claim finds little support in the letter of the law, as was the case with the Singur farmers. But it would be a poor subaltern strategy to rely on the courts only. Political mobilisation and confrontation continue to oftentimes provide a swifter and more efficient route to 'justice' than the slow churning of the wheels of the legal slot machine.

[25] At the time the LF held 235 out of 274 seats in the state assembly.

References

BANERJEE, Parthasarathi
2006 'Land Acquisition and Peasant Resistance at Singur.' *Economic and Political Weekly* 41(46): 4718-20.

BHATTACHARYYA, Dwaipayan
2009 'Of Control and Factions: The Changing 'Party-Society' in Rural West Bengal.' *Economic and Political Weekly* 44(9): 59-69.

BIDWAI, Praful
2008 'Small Car, Big Problems.' *Frontline* 25(3): 117-19.

CALCUTTA HIGH COURT
2008 *Ordering Portion of the Judgment Dated 18th January, 2008*. Kolkata: Calcutta High Court.

CHATTERJEE, Partha
2009 'The Coming Crisis in West Bengal.' *Economic and Political Weekly* 44(9): 42-5.

CHATTOPADHYAY, Suhrid Sankar
2006 'Land Reform not an End in Itself.' *Frontline* 23(25), http://www.flonnet.com/fl2325/stories/20061229001903600.htm (last accessed 15 April 2010).

COHN, Bernard S.
1961 'From Indian Status to British Contract.' *The Journal of Economic History* 21(4): 613-28.
1965 'Anthropological Notes on Disputes and Law in India.' *American Anthropologist* NS 67 (6, part 2): 82-122.
1988 'Some Notes on Law and Change in North India.' Pp. 554-574 in Bernard S. Cohn, *An Anthropologist Among the Historians and Other Essays*. Delhi: Oxford University Press.

GUHA, Abhijit
2007 *Land, Law and the Left: The Saga of Disempowerment of the Peasantry in the Era of Globalisation.* New Delhi: Concept Publishing Company.

GUPTA, Dipankar
2009 *The Caged Phoenix: Can India Fly?* New Delhi: Penguin Viking.

HINDUSTAN TIMES
2007 'Nearly 30 Million cases pending in courts.' 23 May, http://www.hindustantimes.com/News-Feed/india/Nearly-30-million-cases-pending-in-courts/Article1-224578.aspx (last accessed 11 June 2010).

2010 'Check court load before enacting law.' 29 May, http://www.hindustantimes.com/Check-court-load-before-enacting-law/Article1-550453.aspx (last accessed 11 June 2010).

KHARE, R. S.
19 'Indigenous Culture and Lawyer's Law in India.' *Comparative Studies in Society and History* 14(1): 71-96.

KHASNABIS, Rata
2009 'Land Acquisition Act and Social Justice: A Study on Development and Displacement.' Pp. 43-73 in Pradip Kumar Bose and Samir Kumar Das (eds.), *Social Justice and Enlightenment: West Bengal*. New Delhi: Sage.

MADSEN, Stig Toft
n.d. 'Justice and Jihad from the East India Company to the Lashkar-e-Toiba.' Paper delivered at the Focus Asia conference on Interpreting the Rule of Law in Asia, at the Centre for East and South East Asian Studies in Lund, Sweden, 30 March, 2010.

MARSHALL, P.J.
1987 *Bengal: The British Bridgehead*. Cambridge: Cambridge University Press.

METCALF, Thomas R.
1998 *Ideologies of the Raj*. Cambridge: Cambridge University Press.

MOORE, Erin P.
1993 'Gender, Power, and Legal Pluralism: Rajasthan, India.' *American Ethnologist* 20(3): 522-42.

NIELSEN, Kenneth Bo
2008 '"Not on our land!" Peasants' Struggle against Forced Land Acquisition in India's West Bengal.' Pp. 217-46 in Dan Banik (ed.), *Rights and Legal Empowerment in Eradicating Poverty*. Farnham: Ashgate.
2010 'Contesting India's Development? Industrialisation, Land Acquisition and Protest in West Bengal.' *Forum for Development Studies* 37(2): 145-70.

PRAHLADKA, Deepak, Arindam SARKAR and Tapan DAS
2007 'HC Strikes Singur Order.' *Hindustan Times,* 23 February, http://www.hindustantimes.com/News-Feed/newsmartimportedstories/HC-strikes-Singur-order/223974/Article1-205837.aspx (last accessed 22 April 2010).

RAUTRAY, Samanwaya
2010 'SC Singur "Public Purpose" Signal.' *The Telegraph*, 21 April, http://www.telegraphindia.com/1100421/jsp/nation/story_12363325.jsp (last accessed 22 April 2010).

RAY, Gautam (ed.)
2008 *Nandigram and Beyond*. Kolkata: Gangchil.
RAY CHOUDHURY, Ranabir
2008 'Bengal Verdict on Singur.' *The Hindu Business Line*, 21 January, http://www.thehindubusinessline.com/2008/01/21/stories/2008012151000800.htm (last accessed 22 April 2010).
ROBINSON, Nick
2010 'Hard to reach.' *Frontline* 27(3): 46-8.
RUDOLPH, Lloyd I. and Susanne H. RUDOLPH
1965 'Barristers and Brahmans in India: Legal Cultures and Social Change.' *Comparative Studies in Society and History* 8(1): 24-49.
SAMADDAR, Ranabir
2009 'Prescribed, Tolerated and Forbidden Forms of Claim Making.' Pp. 153-179 in Pradip Kumar Bose and Samir Kumar Das (eds.), *Social Justice and Enlightenment: West Bengal*. New Delhi: Sage.
SARKAR, Pradip (ed.)
2007 *The Land Acquisition Act, 1894 with Short Notes along with West Bengal Amendments*. Kolkata: Books-n-books.
SRINIVAS, M. N.
1959 'The Dominant Caste in Rampura.' *American Anthropologist*, NS 61(1): 1-16.
1980 *The Remembered Village*. Berkeley and Los Angeles: University of California Press.
THE STATESMAN
2006 'Buddha's Mantra.' 25 May, http://www.thestatesman.net/index.php?option=com_content&view=article&show=archive&id=151121&catid=42&year=2006&month=5&day=25&Itemid=66 (last accessed 15 April 2010).
THE TIMES OF INDIA
2010 'Courts will take 320 years to clear backlog cases: Justice Rao.' 6 March, http://timesofindia.indiatimes.com/india/Courts-will-take-320-years-to-clear-backlog-cases-Justice-Rao/articleshow/5651782.cms (last accessed 11 June 2010).
VENKATESAN, J
2008 'Supreme Court Refuses to Stay Singur Verdict.' *The Hindu*, 14 May, http://www.thehindu.com/2008/05/14/stories/2008051461241200.htm (last accessed 22 April 2010).

BOOK REVIEW

Marianne O. Nielsen and Robert A. Silverman (eds.), *Criminal Justice in Native America*. Tucson: University of Arizona Press. 2009. 242 pp.

L. Jane McMillan

Veteran editors of several volumes addressing Native and Aboriginal criminal justice issues in North America, Nielson and Silverman specifically commissioned the fourteen chapters in *Criminal Justice in Native America*, this time calling on scholars of Native ancestry to compose about half of the contributions. As in their past collections, the editors retain a minimalist approach using only introductory and concluding chapters to connect the works within. The preface indicates the book is organized in sections; however, the delineation of such sections is absent in the text, but an index catalogues the central themes laid out in the introduction. This compilation sets out to address the consequences of colonialism and the failure of the American criminal justice system to provide justice for Native Americans. Writing from a variety of disciplinary and methodological perspectives, with focuses on law and legislation, crime rates, youth, gender, policing, courts, and corrections, the chapters are organized to provide the reader with an overview of the historical and social context of Native over-involvement with the criminal justice system. Self-determination and adequate resources are the suggested recourses to addressing the crises of oppression, discrimination, racism and overrepresentation experienced by Native Americans as they encounter the justice system. One significant disappointment is that the details and analysis of what self-determination entails, strategies to achieve it, how adequate resources may be acquired and what changes are anticipated, are not addressed.

Silverman's chapter is an expansion of an earlier five-year study to a twenty-one year study that summarizes patterns of crime using the somewhat dubious arrest rates to conclude that Native crime rates are fairly stable, and they tend to follow the patterns of general decline for all Americans. The next three chapters address the inadequacies of the criminal justice system and the problems it in fact exacerbates when Native youth and women come before the law as victims and offenders. In the first of her two chapters Jon'a Meyer highlights the legislation and fiscal restraints that remove the possibility of Native communities to control adjudication of juvenile disputes, force youth into the federal system and eliminate the potential for reaching the rehabilitative and reintegrative goals that are culturally prescribed in Indian Country. The challenges for Native women are laid bare by Fox and Hamby, who both point to the colonial antecedents of victimization and remind the reader that such victimization is not a thing of the past, indeed the contemporary prevalence of violence against Native women is particularly abhorrent and points to ongoing discrimination and oppression. These points are particularly useful for undergraduate student readers trying to grasp systemic discrimination. The authors offer thin outlines of programs, but a more thorough discussion and analysis of the obstacles to prevention and intervention within the context of tribal law, resource shortfalls and self-determination, would be instructive for those more familiar with systemic problems and focused on transforming justice's hegemony.

From Perry's article on hate crime until the conclusion by Nielson, the writing improves and the chapters provide coherent histories and theoretical positions that are supported with empirical evidence. Perry rightly calls for a broader operational definition of hate crime that extends the definition to address the power relations endemic to the act of hate crime as a way to destabilize the normative, institutionalized racial violence that plagues Native life experiences marked by intergenerational grief and trauma. She calls for mobilization around cultural identity and political sovereignty to answer the psychological fallout from federal policies that demeaned culture and used violence to force assimilation and create situations of ongoing segregation in Native America.

The voices of Native America emerge in the discourses and offer important, grounded insights that are too often excluded from volumes where Indigenous experiences are marginalized or ignored. This collection benefits from the inclusion of the authors' local knowledge. Robyn's piece on uranium mining as a state-corporate crime contributes to the growing body of works examining environmental racism and the use of state power, often in violation of treaty rights, to assist the corporate plunder of Indian lands and resources.

Several chapters stand out for their clarity and excellent summaries of the complicated legal histories of Native American justice and reveal the contradictions of jurisdiction and jurisprudence in Indian country that stem from the consequences of colonization and the failure of state recognition of Native entitlements. Cardani's chapter provides a helpful chart summarizing criminal jurisdiction in Indian country and highlights the inconsistencies in rulings as well as the jurisdictional conflicts that interfere and prevent tribal sovereignty. Zion makes another important contribution to his body of work on traditional law and tribal courts as he outlines the historical emergence of tribal courts and delineates the debates central to tribal jurisdiction and court reform. Zion addresses the thorny issues of authenticity, cooptation and adaptation in tribal courts, and speaks to the challenges of evaluating the efficacy of tribal courts using western standards as the instruments to measure performance. Encouragingly he notes a trend toward increasing use of customary law and traditional dispute-resolution methods in tribal courts, but does not give us any insight as to the mechanisms that enhance the legitimacy of such practices for those who administer and use them. Meyer's second piece focuses on tribal justice models and is the stronger of her two contributions; it fits well as a detailed examination of larger questions raised in Zion. Meyer unpacks the concept of peacemaking as processual justice in Navajo country and highlights its significance for maintaining tribal identity and for its potential to transform disputes without romanticizing how peacemaking differentiates tribal justice from its state and federal counterparts.

Two chapters examine the challenges of tribal policing and the problems of using professionalized, adversarial and hierarchical policing approaches in Indian country as they are often at odds with local crime control and restorative justice models and tend to be complicated by assertions of tribal sovereignty. The question raised in the tribal court chapters and also in the context of policing, is this: while there is a critical need for law enforcement services, what are the appropriate formats and can they be used to advance sovereignty, the right to self-government and improve the lives of tribal members? Archambeault's essay on the utility of healing traditions in corrections reveals the contentious issues surrounding the introduction of Native culture, beliefs and healing practices through incarceration. He promotes the potential of using traditional methods and ceremony with offender populations, a subject that will captivate many students.

Generally this text accomplishes its promise to introduce students to the relationships between Native peoples and the prevailing criminal justice system. While it is true that there has been little acknowledgement of the positive contributions of Native Americans to the criminal justice system, this book does not go far enough in explicating those contributions and in demanding state and federal recognition of their value and potential. References to a movement that counters colonization and revitalizes traditional and customary practices are made throughout the text, but the identity of players in the movement are indistinct. The questions of who, what, when, where and how, are not thoroughly expounded. Is there a comprehensive social movement working to establish parallel or alternative justice systems or are Native juridical practices merely experiencing a conurbation within the American Justice system?

The burden of healing the consequences of colonization is placed on Native individuals and communities. These authors point to the responsibility of government to address and dismantle paternalistic relations and systemic discrimination that limit the choices available to Native peoples and cause greater harm as they encounter the justice system. The stories of the political will to empower Native communities and facilitate their achievements in tribal justice through adequate resource allocation and recognition of the efficacy and legitimacy of their practices, both from within and from outside, need to be told again and again. Nielsen and Silverman demonstrate that tribal justice continues to be fettered by the hegemonic American legal system. Arguing that self-determination and adequate resources are the recourses to address the crises of oppression, discrimination, racism and overrepresentation experienced by Native Americans demonstrates that justice, however it is culturally constructed, for Native peoples is elusive and our attention should turn to improving access, supporting alternatives and recognizing assertions of sovereignty.

BOOK REVIEW

Ralph Grillo, Roger Ballard, Alessandro Ferrari André J. Hoekema, Marcel Maussen and Prakash Shah (eds.), *Legal Practice and Cultural Diversity*. Farnham UK and Burlington VT: Ashgate. 2009.

Amy Jackson

The editors assembled the chapters of this collection from papers based on those presented at a conference hosted by the Law School, Queen Mary, University of London in July 2007. The conference was sponsored by the multi-disciplinary research programme International Migration, Integration and Social Cohesion, (IMISCOE) which is a 'network of excellence' funded by the European Commission. One of the principal aims of IMISCOE is to provide a platform for the exchange of innovative ideas related to issues of migration. Due to the emphasis on the exchange of ideas, in comparison to previous collections on law and cultural diversity, such as human rights and culture through anthropological perspectives (Cowan et al. 2001) or immigration in the European context (Shah and Menski 2006), the present collection contributes both a comparative and a theoretical account of the interaction between legal practice and cultural diversity from a range of leading international anthropologists, political scientists and legal specialists.

The collection opens with the Archbishop of Canterbury's statement that scholars and practitioners should consider "the role and rule of law in a plural society of overlapping identities (Williams 2008: 271). The Archbishop made the statement during his comments in February 2008 when he suggested debating the "transformative accommodation" (Shachar 2001) of shari'a councils in the English legal system. His comments were heavily criticised by scholars (Ahmed 2008: 495; Bano 2008). The use of the Archbishop's statement contextualises the contentious nature of the discussions throughout the collection related to whether, and under what conditions, legal systems should acknowledge cultural and religious differences (2). The collection accordingly raises important questions related to

> how contemporary cultural and religious diversity challenges legal practice, how legal practice responds to that challenge and how practice is changing in the encounter with cultural diversity occasioned by large-scale, post-war immigration" (1).

The objective is to consider how legal practice should respond to cultural diversity as both change and challenge the other in various ways. The insights of the collection are beneficial to legal scholars and practitioners for two reasons. It will enable them, first, to gain comparative insights from the experiences and debates surrounding cultural diversity other jurisdictions, and secondly, to understand the theoretical insights that legal pluralism may add to this field of study.

In relation to the comparative insights presented in the collection, several chapters reveal valuable perspectives from the experiences of cultural diversity in an array of jurisdictions. Several authors stress the particular context of each situation. It is still beneficial, however, for legal scholars and practitioners to pose questions about possible comparisons of such experiences and debates. For example, although India is a formerly colonised country with a historical tradition of religious plurality, what could be learned from the Indian notion of secularism as equality of religious pluralism rather than the division of religion from the realm of the state (Menski)? What potential lessons could be learned from the debate in Ontario, Canada related to establishing a Darul-Qada, Muslim Arbitration Tribunal (Bader)? Although Québec holds a particular historical and geopolitical position as a linguistic minority in Canada, what could be learned from the debate related to the doctrine of 'reasonable accommodation' and the recommendations of the report by the Bouchard-Taylor Commission (Gaudreault-DesBiens)? The Dutch constitution places importance on the separation of law from religion, but what could be drawn out from the judicial behaviour which recognises the laws of 'distinct' communities and consequently pluralizes law (Hoekema)? What insights can be gained from a comparative study of North American and European civil cases and the possibility of higher damages being awarded to claimants based on their cultural backgrounds (Renteln)? Finally, what could be learned from the French debate surrounding *laïcité* and multiculturalism, bearing in mind that the French experience strongly differs from that of other European countries (Cohen)?

Legal scholars and practitioners may also benefit from considering the innovative approaches of English legal practice to other situations of cultural diversity. For example, lessons can be learned from the English legal culture's treatment of minority ethnic settlers in other contexts such as African customary laws

(Woodman). It is arguable that Muslim communities should be able to put their beliefs into practice in their daily lives through the frameworks governing European legal orders (Rohe), a view which is reminiscent of that of liberal multicultural theorists (such as Kymlicka 1995). In this regard the particular situation of cultural diversity related to public wearing of the Islamic veil (in its many forms) by women is considered in detail in several other chapters of the collection. For example, the reaction by an English judge to a woman wearing a *Niqab* in a courtroom is presented (Bakht). The European context of the issue of veiling related to the right to manifest religion, under Article 9 European Convention on Human Rights and Fundamental Freedoms 1950, is presented in relation to experiences and contentions in France (de Galembert), and through the subsequent approaches of other European domestic courts (Knights). The way in which freedom to manifest religion under Article 9 has been treated in the English courts following the House of Lords decision in the *Begum* case[1] is further considered in depth (Sandberg). The possibility of learning lessons from these specific experiences and debates is beneficial to scholars and practitioners interested in this area of law.

The collection is also beneficial to legal scholars and practitioners eager to understand the theoretical insights of legal pluralism. Several chapters of the collection allude to the different contexts and ways in which anthropological and socio-legal scholars approach situations of legal pluralism (Benda-Beckmann 2002). For example, one prominent articulation of legal pluralism mentioned in the collection is that of methodological legal pluralism. Thus in his discussion Shah considers the benefits of legal pluralism in relation to current debates surrounding cultural diversity in England. He states that the "Archbishop did not actually use the phrase 'legal pluralism' [in his comments] but he clearly referred to it in several senses of the word 'pluralism' and...[he] would classify him as a legal pluralist" (86). The Archbishop certainly analysed a social situation in which multiple normative orders (such as the laws of the state or those of social associations) operate, interact and conflict with one another within a particular social space (such as within the territory of a nation state) (Griffiths 1986). Shah further states, however, that legal pluralism "has received a more complex" definition than that of the Archbishop's articulation from Chiba and Menski which views "law as an inherently plural and dynamic phenomenon...needing a combination of...approaches to be able to 'see' how it [law] works" (86). For

1 *Regina (SB) v. Governors of Denbigh High School* [2007] 1 AC 100; [2006] UKHL 15 [2006] 2 WLR 719; [2006] HRLR 21.

example Menski, in his discussion in this collection, presents India's plurality-conscious approach to multiculturalism to illustrate how other jurisdictions have responded to the challenges of cultural diversity (Menski). This follows his previous call on scholars to use 'legal methodologies' in order to respond to the challenges of cultural diversity (Menski 2006: 17). He advocated Chiba's approach of a dynamic model of law which held a dual structure of official and unofficial law as well as legal postulates (the three-level structure of law) which adhered to the plurality-conscious approach to law (Chiba 1986: 4; Menski 2006: 19). The benefit of methodological legal pluralism for scholars and practitioners interested in the relationship between cultural diversity and the law is that the use of a plurality of legal methods illuminates the complexity of normative orders within a social space, rather than establishing that several normative orders simply exist within a social space. Another approach to legal pluralism mentioned in the collection, presented by Hoekema, is the notion of 'inter-legality' proposed by De Sousa Santos (2002). Inter-legality is a process rather than an outcome where "elements of a dominant legal order [or a normative order], both national and international and ... the frames of meaning that constitute these orders, [are adopted] into the practice of a local legal order and/or the other way round" (191-192). The approach stipulates that different normative orders cannot be said to have a separate existence from one another, but rather are interconnected. The benefit of inter-legality for scholars and practitioners is the introduction of a dynamic process to situations of legal pluralism, rather than a dynamic approach to law, as advocated by Chiba and Menski.

It is contended that a notion of homogeneous cultures and normative orders is assumed by the articulations of legal pluralism mentioned in the collection. For example, the foundational chapter of the collection, which presents an overview of the challenges and accommodation of cultural diversity in law, asserts that "[r]esolving competing demands and entitlements grounded in a plurality of legal orders [or normative orders], themselves multiple, cross-cutting and internally complex is never a straightforward task" (Ballard, Ferrari, Grillio, Hoekema, Maussen and Shah: 25). The statement *prima facie* refers to the heterogeneous nature of normative orders as the notion of homogeneous cultures and normative orders is assumed in the chapter. For example, the research of Bano into women's experiences of family law related to the proceedings of shari'a councils is cited in the chapter (2008). Her research responds to the Archbishop's comments, finding that "the view that Muslims increasingly seek freedom to live under shari'a is not only extremely problematic", which she evidences by capturing the experiences of Muslim women in relation to the councils through their narratives, but also that such an approach "fails to capture the complexity of British Muslim identity as fragmented, porous and hybrid" (2008: 309). Bano's research highlights two important issues. The first relates to the potential for gender discrimination in the establishment of shari'a councils under English law. The second issue relates to the fact that there is no homogeneous British Muslim identity. In relation to the potential for gender discrimination it is stated in the chapter that Bano's research "throws much light on the complex relationship of women to [shari'a] councils... [Consequently] 'accommodation' may mean conceding to patriarchal interests" (Ballard, Ferrari, Grillio, Hoekema, Maussen and Shah: 24). It is merely argued that gender discrimination may have to be conceded in order to uphold cultural diversity, without any further discussion of the reasons for this. Moreover, the lack of a homogeneous identity of a cultural group is also given no detailed discussion other than the mention that normative orders are multiple, cross-cutting and internally complex. This situation could have been further evidenced by referring to the *Begum* case (for example, where respected scholars disagreed as to the particular level of modest dressing which an Islamic woman should practice (*Begum* case: paras. 13-14)) or even through further discussion of Bano's own work. This would have been beneficial as, in comparison to the question as to which normative orders may be interacting within a particular social space (the question posed by the Archbishop), Bano further questioned what claims Muslim women, confronted by claims of different normative orders, made in their own lives. This type of reasoning reflects the 'critical' legal pluralist question which turns the traditional agency pattern inside out (Kleinhans and Macdonald 1997: 46). Posing both the former and the latter questions challenges the assumption of a homogeneous or essentialised notion of culture and normative orders. Such an approach is non-essential as it points towards normative orders being internally complex due to legal subject's own understanding of their subjectivity or legal identity. It is contended that the collection would have benefited from further discussion of the approach taken by Bano.

The collection concludes with an important theoretical discussion on whether human rights, in the context of ethnic plurality, are always a vehicle for liberation (Ballard). Ballard focuses on family law. He argues that one of the most *serious lacunae* in the human rights discourse is "its failure to take cognizance of one of the most salient features of the human condition, our capacity to order our inter-personal relationships on the basis of our own self-constructed conceptual premises" (301). His argument is that the self-construction of a person's own normative orders is not considered by scholars concerned with human rights. Other discussions in the collection could have benefited from considering Ballard's approach. Furthermore, the self-construction of normativity is considered in Bano's approach.

Overall, the collection adequately responds to the Archbishop of Canterbury's statement quoted in the introductory chapter. The role and rule of law is illustrated in various ways and from a range of multicultural societies to depict how it is changed and challenged by cultural diversity and *visa versa.* Although the experiences recorded and the surrounding debates are context specific, it is beneficial for legal scholars and practitioners to contemplate the possible comparisons. The collection is also beneficial for scholars and practitioners interested to gain further understanding of the theoretical insights of legal pluralism. However, in relation to the Archbishop's statement referring to the consideration of overlapping identities in plural societies, the collection is on the one hand successful in highlighting the range of contexts and ways in which scholars within various disciplines define law and legal pluralism. On the other hand, the collection could have presented a more detailed discussion of Bano's research which captured the complexity of British Muslim identity as fragmented, porous and hybrid. Discussion of the complexities of religious identity, as highlighted in the *Begum* case which illuminated the fact that there can be many different interpretations of religious practices, would also have been beneficial for the collection in order to defeat any possible presumption of homogeneous cultures or normative orders. Furthermore, consideration of Ballard's concluding remarks, that it is important for scholars to question the self-construction of a person's own normativity, would also have also overcome any presuppositions of the existence of homogeneous cultural groups. Whether the collection is successful in considering the nature of overlapping *identities* in multicultural societies depends on how one interprets the terms 'legal pluralism' and legal 'identity'.

References

AHMED, Sameer

2008 'Pluralism in British Islamic Reasoning: The Problem with Recognizing Islamic Law in the United Kingdom.' *Yale Journal of International Law* 33: 491-497.

BANO, Samia

2008 'In Pursuit of Religious and Legal Diversity: A Response to the Archbishop of Canterbury and the 'Shar'ia Debate' in Britain'.

Ecclesiastical Law Journal 10: 282–309.

BENDA-BECKMANN, von Franz

2002 'Who's Afraid of Legal Pluralism?' *Journal of Legal Pluralism* 37: 37-82.

CHIBA, Masaji (ed.)

1986 *Asian Indigenous Law in Interaction with Received Law*. London: KPI.

COWAN, Jane.K., Marie-Bénédict DEMBOUR and Richard, A. WILSON (eds.)

2001 *Culture and Rights: Anthropological Perspectives*. Cambridge: Cambridge University Press.

GRIFFITHS, John

1986 'What is Legal Pluralism?' *Journal of Legal Pluralism* 24: 1–55.

KLEINHANS, Martha-Marie and Roderick A. MACDONALD

1997 'What is a Critical Legal Pluralism?' *Canadian Journal of Law and Society* 12(2): 25–46.

KYMLICKA, Will

1995 *Multicultural Citizenship: A Liberal Theory of Minority Rights*. Oxford: Clarendon Press.

MENSKI, Werner

2006 'Rethinking Legal Theory in Light of Migration.' Pp. 13-28 in Prakash Shah and Werner Menski (eds.), *Migration, Diasporas and Legal Systems in Europe*. London: Routledge-Cavendish.

SANTOS, Boaventura de Sousa

2002 *Towards a New Legal Common Sense. Law, Globalization, and Emancipation*. London: Butterworths.

SHAH, Prakash and Werner MENSKI (eds.)

2006 *Migration, Diasporas and Legal Systems in Europe*. Abingdon: Routledge-Cavendish.

SHACHAR, Ayelet

2001 *Multicultural Jurisdictions; Cultural Differences and Women's Rights*. Cambridge: Cambridge University Press.

WILLIAMS, Rowan

2008 'Civil and Religious Law in England: A Religious Perspective.' *Ecclesiastical Law Journal* 10: 262–282.

BOOK REVIEW

Janine Ubink, André J. Hoekema and Willem J. Assies (eds.), *Legalising Land Rights. Local Practices, State Responses and Tenure Security in Africa, Asia and Latin America*. Leiden: Leiden University Press. 2009. 618 pp.

Christian Lund

Millions of people live and work on land they do not legally own. This often puts them in a precarious situation. However, waves of land reforms in Africa, Asia and Latin America intended to make property more secure have often had the perverse effect of undermining whatever tenure security poorer people experience. *Legalising Land Rights* is a welcome effort to take stock of recent policies and developments.

Two general trends in legalisation of land rights have dominated the scene over the past decades. On the one hand, state-led individual titling and registration characterised efforts to legalise possession and create property. Such policies have been based on assumptions that individual property rights are crucial to insure that landholders have incentives to invest in improvement of their production, crucial to create collateral for credit, and crucial to make sure that the most productive agents have access to the means of production, most importantly: land. Policies inspired by these ideas often intended to 'replace' customary ownership with modern property. While policies of individual titling enjoyed some success (a few famous studies (from Thailand and China) are always put forth as evidence), a long list of disappointing experiences also saw the light of day. Registration programmes have often proved slow, expensive, difficult to keep up-to-date and hard for poor people to access, and access to credit has not simply resulted from formalisation of landed property (Shipton 2009). Moreover, research began to show that some customary forms of tenure actually provided tenure security, even if it was not formalised and individualised according to the conventional index of the 'Western World'. This fuelled contrasting and more recent efforts from the 1980s onwards to think in terms of formalising customary forms of possession, not replacing custom, but elevating it to law. However, custom is rarely equitable or fair, and formalisation often meant consolidation of the position of the already powerful in society. A third movement took hold in the early 2000s with the backing of multiple diverse international donor agencies. It attempted to reconcile a national legal framework with local land rights and allocation processes. *Legalising Land Rights* is an analysis of some of the experiences of these policies. The policies were propelled by the idea that land reform should be decentralised and if possible avoid the active involvement of a removed and corrupt central government, and it generally favoured the idea that land transactions should ideally be private and not involve the public (Borras and Franco 2009; Sikor and Müller 2009). One of the most policy-influential books on property and land in recent years arguing in this vein is *The Mystery of Capital* (de Soto 2000). The author drives a very forceful argument that the state should secure and guarantee and formalise as private property the land that the small in society already possess under customary arrangements in order to enable them to produce, have, and control capital. De Soto's work has incurred praise as well as criticism for its simplicity. However, whereas de Soto's idea works from the confident assumption that the state exists as a set of congruent and hegemonic institutions capable of enforcing one particular interpretation of property, *Legalising Land Rights* takes a path less travelled where catchy statements are not purchased at the expense of nuance and where such assumptions are questioned rather than taken as 'principles true in every country'. This is the major strength of the book. Property is not dissociated from governance, nor law from power, nor rights from politics.

The book consists of some nineteen case studies from Ethiopia, Ghana, Namibia, Senegal, Bolivia, Mexico, China and Indonesia. Each country forms the context for two or three chapters. This permits a more than usually thorough discussion of the individual country-cases. The many cases offer opportunities to analyse the different configurations of 'extra-legal' ownership and the challenges these produce for legalisation. It is not a simple affair. If a silver bullet existed, it almost certainly would have been fired by now. Frustration with the complexity of land related problems may render decision-makers susceptible to 'clear-cut', 'once-and-for-all', seemingly 'obvious solutions'. Their enthusiasm for simple directives is understandable. But simplistic policies have a truly poor record in Africa, Asia and Latin America. However, inaction and refusal to deal with land issues politically is not a real option. 'Autonomous' land dynamics have significant socio-economic and political effects, not all of which are benign. There is no 'natural evolution' of land tenure systems; they are integral parts of social and political processes, and it is in this respect that the case studies demonstrate their power of illumination. A sobering observation stemming from the series of case studies is that efforts to reconcile the pluralism of custom with more uniform principles of governance are not new. Colonialism, as a project of state formation, signalled the first efforts to legalise and homogenize. Principles of legal integration - even in areas with putative indirect rule – have been given effect in many different ways ranging from subtle to violent. The case chapters seem to suggest that it is only if current policy efforts to legalise land rights are understood in an historical perspective that they can be conducted with the modesty that the immensity of such a task demands. Another inference drawn from the cases is that while the legal status of land is important, it is not the only – and sometimes not even the most – important factor in securing people's livelihood. Simple things such as the quality and quantity of the resources secured by law are not trivial. The cases also demonstrate how legal innovation (in China) with small incremental steps may change, and legalise, the terms of tenure. This raises the question of whose interests are served in this process and what happens in situations where formalisation and legalisation improves government actors' possibilities for acquisition of ordinary people's land. The question of legalisation is not merely – sometimes not even primarily – a legal question (Hsing, 2010).

Legal pluralism is more than an omnipresent societal phenomenon; it is also its epistemological consequence, namely a dogged insistence on the empirical data even – or maybe especially – if it does not conform to ideational models or ply neatly into policy. The editors, all scholars who have contributed substantially to the development and consolidation of the field of legal pluralism in their own right, have collected and edited a bundle of highly readable sticks of scholarship. It displays immense variety, not only in circumstance, but also in people's and governments' responses to the challenge of legislation in diversity. It might easily have belied this richness had the editors been tempted to draw general substantive conclusions on the basis of the contributions. Grounded reasoning is the salt of the analysis of legal pluralism. Nonetheless, it seems that the collection could have provided an underpinning for the identification some generic areas of contention – politico-legal pressure points, if you will - in a fluid and variegated world engaging in the stickiness of legalisation. Such efforts could serve to establish systematic analytical approaches for scholars and practitioners alike. However, to do that might have been in conflict with the general pressure to go into publication as rapidly as possible - a regrettable trend, which unfortunately it seems impossible to stem. This said however, the collection is inspirational in its ambition to display some of the challenges in fostering legislative strategies that may arbitrate between state perspectives and local land rights.

References

BORRAS JR., Saturnino M., and Jennifer C. FRANCO
2009 *Transnational Agrarian Movements Struggling for Land and Citizenship Rights,* IDS Working Paper 323. Brighton, UK: Institute of Development Studies, University of Sussex.

DE SOTO, Hernando
2000 *The Mystery of Capital: Why Capitalism Triumphs in the West and Fails Everywhere Else.* New York: Basic Books.

HSING, You-tien
2010 *The Great Urban Transformation. Politics of Land and Property in China.* Oxford: Oxford University Press.

SHIPTON, Parker
2009 *Mortgaging the Ancestors. Ideologies of Attachment in Africa.* New Haven and London: Yale University Press.

SIKOR, Thomas and Daniel MÜLLER
2009 'The limits of state-led land reform.' *World Development* 37: 1307-16.

BOOK REVIEW

Fernanda Pirie, *Peace and Conflict in Ladakh: The construction of a fragile web of order*. Brills Tibetan Studies Library, Vol. 13. Leiden, Boston: Brill. 2007

Judith Beyer

Fernanda Pirie's *Peace and conflict in Ladakh* is an anthropological monograph about rural life in northernmost India. Her book is based on extensive periods of fieldwork in this part of the Himalayan mountain range, supplemented by historical and comparative research on Tibet where she worked previously. The book is well-written and enjoyable to read. It includes two maps and several colored photographs, as well as a glossary and an index. The main questions Pirie tries to answer in her book are laid out clearly in the introduction: First, what are the Ladakhis' constructed ideas of community and social order? Second, how do the Ladakhis maintain their social order? Third, why do the Ladakhis place interests of their community above their own rights? And fourth, what role does Buddhism play in the maintenance of social order? (1-9)

In chapter two Pirie gives a historical overview of Ladakh, focusing on legal developments in this region from the eighth century onwards. While different systems of governance were imposed on the rural population throughout the centuries, Pirie emphasizes that people in the remote areas of Ladakh have always tried to decide community matters, particularly internal disputes, autonomously from state officials and the Ladakhi kings. Surprisingly, this reservation also concerns the local monasteries and individual Buddhist leaders. Pirie argues that, while Buddhism forms an integral part of Ladakhi culture, it is kept separate from village affairs. She speaks of a "dual system" (28) of secular and religious power and authority, which she continues to explore throughout the book.

In chapter three she introduces her actual fieldsite, a mountain community of two hundred inhabitants, the village of Photoksar. Here the reader learns about the villagers' social institutions such as the two kinds of household units (*khangba* and *khangu*), the village council (*yulpa*), and its agent, the headman (*goba*), and a ranking system called *dralgo*, which manifests itself in the way seats are arranged during any social occasion. The chapter also deals with customary regulations, issues of hierarchy and equality, leadership and autonomy, and ways of social sanctioning such as shaming (*trelba*). Pirie argues that villagers have a strong antipathy towards individualism. Equality is promoted by the pressures to conform to people's expectations and to downplay personal status and superiority.

Chapter four shows how these concepts are put into practice once conflict arises in the village. By means of several case studies Pirie explores how and by whom disputes are mediated, and she looks into the epistemology of conflict, that is, the emic perspective on what a conflict is and how it should be dealt with. She concludes that disputes between individuals are always viewed as posing "danger to the order of the community requiring resolution and the ceremonial restoration of good relations." (87)

In chapter five Pirie investigates religion, and particularly the spiritual realm, concluding that "neither the moral order of Buddhism nor the realm of the spirits is related to the moral and political order of the village" (90). She summarizes her conclusion by stating that the villagers' ritual practices are often determined by pragmatic concerns, while the moral and ritual content of religious texts as proclaimed by monks serve ethical purposes "which the villagers admire, but do not regard as efficacious to deal with their own troublesome numina" (108). Through a critique of authors who have attributed too much social significance to the moral codes of monastic Buddhism, Pirie argues that the monastic elite and the Ladakhi villagers not only live in different geographical and social worlds, but also in different epistemological worlds.

Chapter six is a description of a ritual called *Losar*, which celebrates the new year. During this ritual established social relations and moral ways of conduct between male and female and between old and young are juxtaposed or become exaggerated, caricatured, or transgressed. According to Pirie, *Losar* triggers conflictual dynamics between the village council (*yulpa*) and the resident monks, between villagers and non-villagers, as well as the villagers' "self-conscious suspicion of modernity and resistence [sic] to change" (112). Driving out the evil spirits of the old year, the village community temporarily suspends "the normal world and its social order" (120). This event, on which Pirie has rich ethnographic data, is interpreted in the tradition of classic symbolic anthropology, namely as a rite of passage where "[t]he festival represents the undoing of the well-established pattern of the village's social and political order as much as it affirms it" (120).

Chapter seven explores what Pirie calls "the sacred social order", echoing

Durkheim's concept of the sacred social community. Since there is no word for the concept of "order" as such in the local language, she looks at what villagers say when a dispute has come to an end: "It is OK again." She suggests that the idea behind such utterances is to achieve dispute settlement and not "abstract justice" but still argues that there is an "implicit notion of order underlying such concerns" (125). Pirie states that for the Ladakhis "[t]he social and moral order of the community in Photoksar is, therefore, defined by the notion of the ideal community in which everyone lives harmonious lives. The social is sacred" (128).

Chapter eight is a comparative chapter in which Pirie assesses how neighboring Tibet influenced legal developments in Ladakh. Reviewing historical sources and academic literature on this subject, she comes to the conclusion that, while Tibet and Ladakh do not form "a single, coherent, let alone Buddhist, cultural system" (167), certain cultural patterns resonate, such as "a certain attitude to leadership and centralised judicial control" (169).

In chapter nine Pirie looks at broad political changes currently happening in urban Ladakh, such as the establishment of new administrative and religious bodies for dispute settlement. These also begin to impact on rural areas as factions emerge and new forms of organization and control are introduced. But while "[t]hese new systems are undoubtedly forces for change" she concludes that "the old pattern of deference and distance towards external influences remains" (195).

In her conclusion Pirie summarizes her argument that a sense of order underlies judicial processes in her fieldsite, which becomes manifest in the villagers' understanding that living together in harmony is the ultimate rationale to which individual interests have to be subordinated. Within this "sacred social space", as Pirie calls it, Buddhism plays no central role. Not only Buddhist thoughts, but also other external (e.g., administrative) influences are kept separate from this sphere. Despite this resistance, "new instances of the sacred social" are created in the face of increasing globalization and modernization, leading to "a composite political order" (Geertz) on "the local level." To deal with this contradictory dynamic, Pirie suggests that "[t]he insights of Durkheim and Geertz need to be brought together ... to make sense of the way in which order is constructed and maintained amidst the complex pattern of political, economic and religious forces that characterises contemporary Ladakh" (207).

For me, Pirie's most intriguing argument, based on her own ethnographic data of the villagers' ritual practices as described in chapters five and six, is that the villagers have maintained a "secular morality" (105) quite separate from Buddhist values. In addition to this stimulating suggestion, which casts doubts on seemingly established views on the role of Buddhism in everyday life, the data in these chapters is outstanding because Pirie herself participated in the events she so richly describes, whereas much of her data on dispute settlement is limited to conversations with villagers about such cases. As a woman, she chose not to take part in the all-male *yulpa* meetings, for instance, and when a mediator was called in to settle an argument between members of her host family (79), her distanced description gives rise to the impression that she, in fact, did not personally attend the negotiations. As a result, her analysis of "peace and conflict" gives priority to accounts of how life in Ladakh *should be* ordered. Whenever her informants do tell her how little they listen to the village council and how quarrelsome they in fact are (e.g., 126), Pirie deduces from such statements that villagers must have an underlying "sense of order", and that their practices and discourses aim to maintain such an "order". Throughout she privileges normative statements on the importance of harmony and formal acts of reconciliation over individuals' unresolved and lingering conflicts: in one case, she stops her discussion even though the two individuals who had begun the dividing argument "remained on bad terms", just because the two households involved claimed to have restored their "good relations" (79, 82). Thus the reader increasingly gets the impression that what Pirie deduces from the villagers' negative appraisal of conflict is her own "implicit idea of order" (e.g., 125, 186).

If "order" is not a concept her informants talk about nor anything which could be observed as visibly guiding their actions, and if the explicit goal of the villagers' actions is not abstract justice but to achieve a settlement, as she states herself, what do we gain by calling these processes "the construction of a fragile web of order"? Methodologically, it remains unresolved how one can grasp people's "implicit idea of order". Pirie's further differentiation into social, biological, moral, political, legal, cosmological, and religious "order" adds to its arbitrariness.

Notwithstanding this specific criticism, the book succeeds in providing a thorough, well-structured account of the social organization of rural Ladakh, which also takes account of more regional entanglements. The ethnographic depth is remarkable throughout and gives evidence of Pirie's intimate knowledge of the area. Her exploration of "secular morality" opens up new ways of assessing the role of Buddhism in law and society, in and beyond Ladakh. For these virtues "Peace and conflict in Ladakh" will be of interest to anthropologists, scholars of law and religion, and everybody interested in the region.

BOOK REVIEW

Amanda Perreau-Saussine and James Bernard Murphy (eds.), *The Nature of Customary Law: Legal, Historical and Philosophical Perspectives*. Cambridge: Cambridge University Press. 2007. ix + 338 pp.

Gordon R. Woodman

In the past century scholarly study of the many past and present varieties of customary law has grown considerably. There is now a stock of information, and many descriptive and analytical theories, about a range of customary laws, including those of the peoples who form the majority populations of African and Asian countries, of indigenous minorities in North and South America, Australasia and India, of immigrant minorities in countries of the North, of groups engaged in long-term commercial activities locally and internationally, of other economic groups such as members of professions and groups of co-workers, of residents in particular localities, and of groups such as political parties and religious communities, as well as of the customary elements of state laws, religious laws, transnational laws and international law. The literature contains discussion of theoretical questions such as which of these varieties may be classified as laws, how if at all they may be legitimately changed, and what is their relationship to various types of morality.

The title of this book promises to make a contribution to this theory. But at its start a puzzle emerges. The introductory summary (i, repeated on the back outer cover) claims: "Nowhere are customary rules of law more prominent than in international law". It is difficult to find a ground on which it can be claimed that customary law is exceptionally prominent in international law or that international law comprises a large part of the field of customary law. The book is not quite as narrow as this preliminary statement suggests. The editors state in their introduction that the studies in the book also focus on the common law, and further, that "customary practices underpin *every* legal system" (their emphasis), especially in the form of rules of interpretation (9-10). But even here, by the words "every legal system" they seem to mean no more than every *state* or international legal system. The subject matter does not include the vast range of non-state manifestations of customary law.

A book on the theory of customary law might be expected to base its arguments on specific instances of customary laws which demonstrably exist or have existed. Social scientific research has provided accounts of many. Although there are references to lessons which might be learnt "from philosophy, from psychology, from behavioral economics, and from other disciplines and sub-disciplines that can help us to make sense of the process by which customary law is created and interpreted..." (18, in the chapter by Frederick Shauer), the book ignores the sub-discipline of legal anthropology. Nowhere in this book is there a reference to the writings on customary laws by Collier, the Comaroffs, Evans-Pritchard, Gluckman, Greenhouse, Hoebel, Holleman, Macaulay, Malinowski, Meek, Merry, Moore, Nader, Pospisil, Rattray, Rosen, Schapera, Starr, Strathern, van Vollenhoven or the von Benda-Beckmanns - to mention only the first 20 or so which happen to come to mind. There is one reference to Bohannan (18), but not to his *Justice and Judgement Among the Tiv* (Bohannan 1957). There is one reference to Fallers (at 18, Fallers 1969). It is claimed that there have been few theoretical investigations of customary law (e.g. at i), but no contributor appears to have noticed the significant contributions to the theory of customary law of Ehrlich, John Griffiths, Merry or Vanderlinden, as well as virtually all of the other writers just listed.

Perhaps the contributors would reply that they are engaged in theoretical or conceptual analysis, not in the formulation of social-scientific hypotheses. The answer to that is that no theory about law, however pure and remote from contingent facts, can be formulated without taking as true some propositions, however minimal, about laws as social facts. Essays about the characteristics of customary law must be based on reliable information about at least one customary law, and essays on the nature of customary law in general must convey knowledge of at least the main varieties, and arguably should take account of all varieties of the phenomenon. This book is based on far too slender a foundation of explicit knowledge for it to contribute significantly to understanding of the topic of its title.

Nevertheless the papers provide interesting discussion of certain aspects of the two types of customary law mentioned, and insights into some literature in legal philosophy. They fall into three categories: analyses of the relevance of fundamental theoretical questions to customary law; studies of the status of customary law in common law systems; and studies of the place of customary law in international law. Here I concentrate on the first, making brief comments on the others.

The discussions of theory relate certain issues of customary law to classical philosophy and modern legal theory. Thus James Bernard Murphy's chapter, entitled 'Habit and convention at the foundation of custom', is concerned primarily with the use made of the concepts of customary law, habit and convention in leading literature of philosophical jurisprudence. He shows that from Plato to Kelsen jurisprudence

> rests upon three fundamental concepts of order and three allied concepts of law: the order intrinsic to human nature grounds the natural law, the order found in informal social practices grounds the customary law, and deliberately stipulated order grounds enacted law (53).

He examines the implications of this for theory, with an especially illuminating discussion of concepts of nature (*phusei*), habit (*ethei*) and teaching (*didakē*) in the philosophy of Aristotle (55-56). This leads to a consideration of the disputed relationship between law in general and custom. He suggests a distinction between discussions of habit and of convention:

> ... most jurists list custom as one among several independent sources of law, but the jurists of the historical school often assert that all law is custom.... If we are focused on conventions, then custom is but one source of our legal conventions; but if we are focused on habits of tacit knowledge and skill, then all law rests upon custom, in the sense that the interpretation and application of law rest upon deep reservoirs of tacit know-how" (66-67).

From here he argues that "the growth of law [of all types] means the growth of custom" (67, having cited Ellickson 1991). This enables him to engage in reflection on more modern writers, including James Carter, Hayek, Raz and Finnis. He counters the Austinian, and still quite prevalent view that "particular customs are not lawful until a court enforces them" by the succinct conclusion that "rather, a court enforces them because, as a class of customs meeting established legal criteria, they are regarded as already lawful" (77). He concludes with a reflection on the significance of custom for legal theory and legal philosophy (78). While it may be mistaken to claim that there has been a neglect of theory in studies of customary law, Murphy appears correct to criticize the literature of general jurisprudence for its neglect of customary law.

Ross Harrison examines the relationship between convention (by which he means what the English lawyer would call local custom) and morality. In his subtle argument he contends that, while morality is more than mere convention, it is necessarily related to convention, and that the recognition of conduct as conventional does not remove its moral force. Jean Porter provides a perspicacious study of the place of custom, legislation and natural right in Gratian's *Decretum* of the 12th century. Brian Tierney demonstrates the importance attached by Suarez, writing in the late 16th and early 17th centuries, to customary law in the formation of international and other law. He also discusses the work of Vitoria, but this, while interesting on questions of human rights and general morality in law, is not shown to contain much of importance on customary law.

Christoph Kletzer provides an informative study of "the philosophic ground of the Hegel-Savigny controversy". Especially interesting is the account of Savigny's "decisively anti-philosophical stance" (130). That scholar's doctrine of legal sources defined all law as positive law, which was already in existence before problems about legal relations could arise. Law was not voluntarily created by a formal legal authority, but, for the would-be legal philosopher, was simply given (131). It lived in the consciousness of the *Volk* (132), having been created by the "inner, silently-working forces" of that consciousness (134, quoting Savigny 1967: 13). Consistently with this, Kletzer summarises Savigny's view as: "Custom itself is not law and the positive law owes nothing to custom" (134). What Savigny referred to as "so-called customary law" (134, quoting Savigny 1967: 14) might provide indirect knowledge of a community's positive law for the outsider, but for members of the community "their cognition [of positive law] is an *immediate* one, based only on direct intuition" (134, quoting Savigny 1840: 38).

These chapters, by keeping their discussions of customary law at a general level, say much of interest about legal philosophy in general, but less about customary law. Frederick Schauer, in a chapter on "Pitfalls in the interpretation of customary law", engages in more questionable argument. His paper is carefully limited to questions about the process of interpreting acts and decisions for the purpose of determining the content of customary laws. Moreover, it does not attempt to answer these questions, but rather to clarify them. However, the discussion is also limited to a few sets of instances, namely, "the role of customary law in common law adjudication [and this means only in adjudication in the common law of

England]... and the role of customary international law as a part of international law more generally" (14). He argues that customary law, which he limits to customary systems which are recognised in "formal law", that is, in state or international law, must be seen as being developed from "pre-legal" normative practices, not from other types of regularities of conduct (18). Recognition of this would indeed clarify the analysis of state court decisions in multicultural societies, by distinguishing clearly between cases in which the courts consider whether to apply norms of non-state customary law and those in which they consider whether to take facts of a minority culture into account when applying general state law. However, Schauer's illustration of this issue is difficult to follow. He refers to the English case *Mercer v. Denne* [1905] 2 Ch 538, in which, as he says, "it was held ... that the fishermen of Walmer were entitled by a local custom to dry their nets on a particular stretch of sand", an act which would otherwise have been a trespass (quoting Cross 1977: 162). He then states that "there is no indication that the customary practice was done under claim of right, and no indication that the practice itself became normative", and "[a] fisherman new to the Walmer area would not have been subject to criticism, we suppose, for not participating in the custom...." (19). But all three judgments in the Court of Appeal referred to the practice as being, according to custom, the exercise of a right, thus placing it in a normative category. The imagined case of a fisherman who did not take advantage of the custom and was not criticised for this is irrelevant. The normative aspect of the custom was not the imposition of a duty on fishermen, but rather the conferment of a privilege on them. A more satisfactory analysis of this custom would place it in the context of a body of interrelated normative customs: there was a general customary obligation to observe property rights conferred by state law, but in this case a specific customary right had arisen which constituted an exception to this. Again one suspects that an engagement with more numerous instances of practised customary laws would have avoided puzzlement over this case.

Schauer then analyses certain questions posed by various philosophers in order to illuminate the decisions which may be made in cases which consider customary laws. Virtually all are discussed in terms of decisions by English common law courts, and so are discussions of the circumstances in which these courts will recognize customary laws. Thus the discussion of 'Llewellyn's question' (28-31) considers whether for every instance in which there are grounds for holding the relevant customary law to comprise one particular norm, there are also tenable grounds for holding it to be a norm of different content. This discussion refers to Llewellyn's rule-skeptical early work (Llewellyn 1930) and to his later analysis of the judicial process (Llewellyn 1960). It also suggests the important observation that norms involved in litigated, hard cases are not the entirety, nor even a large portion of the norms of a legal system. It notes that the existence of conflicting norms on a particular issue is an empirical question. But it fails to mention Llewellyn's own empirical study in collaboration with Hoebel of the customary law of the Cheyenne Indians (Llewellyn and Hoebel 1941), which could have been used to formulate a plentiful number of illustrations of the question.

Three chapters are within the second category of this book, studies of aspects of the relationship of customary law to common law doctrine. David Ibbetson, on "Custom in medieval law" considers the uses of the idea of custom in England, comparing these with the practices in western mainland Europe. His conclusion, after a study of medieval literature on the common law, and court records, is that "within the medieval legal tradition custom can be seen as a form of safety valve enabling courts to derogate from the common law when there was sufficient pressure [from those subject to the law] to do so" (174). Alan Cromartie's chapter on "The idea of common law as custom" is largely a collection of reports on and ideas about custom in English legal literature from 1066 to Blackstone. Various views as to the nature of "custom" emerge from this, and in particular the distinction between popular custom (custom practised generally by the people) and custom as made or declared by judges. An interesting comparison might be made between that distinction and the distinction drawn today in various terminological forms between living law and officially recognised, or lawyers' customary law. Michael Lobban, in the first part of his chapter on "Custom, common law reasoning and the law of nations in the nineteenth century", considers the views of English lawyers on the nature of general customs, local customs and the custom of merchants (257-264). In the second part of his chapter he applies these findings to the attitudes of judges to international law.

The other four chapters are concerned with customary international law. Randall Lesaffer contributes a chapter on "Siege warfare in the early modern age: a study on the customary laws of war". This is a study of texts written approximately in the century before and the century after the Treaty of Westphalia, 1648, revealing the writers' understanding of these customary laws which could on occasion dramatically limit the unrestrained use of violence in war. Amanda Perreau-Saussine, in "Three ways of writing a treatise on public international law: textbooks and the nature of customary international law", takes a number of modern text-writers on international law, and examines the extent to which they assert a natural law or rely on customary practice to establish principles of international law. Gerald J. Postema, in a chapter on "Custom in international law: a normative practice account" devotes most of the discussion to a consideration of the customs followed by individuals in a society. This is not a report of empirical research, but seems to be soundly based on a tacit knowledge and understanding of empirical facts. Only in the last section does the paper argue for the applicability of such customs in international law. John Tasioulas, in the final chapter, on "Customary international law and the quest for global justice" is concerned with the prospects for the reform of international law in order to secure greater justice, that is, to bring it more fully into accord with moral norms. He contends that this may be achieved through arguments based on customary international law, as conceived by him. It is helpful to the general student of customary law, as also to the student of international law.

This collection presents insights into the arguments and conclusions of certain leading philosophers, provides information about the attitudes in the past of common lawyers to custom, and contributes to the understanding of customary international law. But it does not advance understanding of the nature of customary law.

References

BOHANNAN, Paul
1957 *Justice and Judgement Among the Tiv*, London: Oxford University Press for the International African Institute.
CROSS, Rupert
1977 *Precedent in English Law*, 3rd ed. Oxford: Clarendon Press.
ELLIKSON, Robert
1991 *Order Without Law: How Neighbors Settle Disputes*. Cambridge MA: Harvard UP.
FALLER, LLOYD A.
1969 *Law Without Precedent: legal ideas in action in the courts of colonial Busoga*. Chicago: Chicago University Press.
LLEWELLYN, Karl N.
1930 *The Bramble Bush: Some Lectures on Law and its Study*. New York: Columbia University School of Law.
1960 *The Common Law Tradition: Deciding Appeals*. Boston: Little Brown.
LLEWELLYN, Karl N., and E. Adamson HOEBEL

1941 *The Cheyenne Way: Conflict and Case Law in Primitive Jurisprudence*. Norman: University of Oklahoma Press.

SAVIGNY, Friedrich Carl von

1840 *System des heutigen Römischen Rechts [System of Modern Roman Law]*. Berlin: Veit.

1967 *Vom Beruf unserer Zeit für Gesetzgebung und Rechtswissenschaft [On the Vocation of our Age for Legislation and Jurisprudence]* (first published 1812, Berlin). Hildesheim: Georg Olms.